CAMPAIGN 370

LEYTE GULF 1944 (1)

The Battles of the Sibuyan Sea and Samar

MARK STILLE

ILLUSTRATED BY JIM LAURIER

Series editor Nikolai Bogdanovic

OSPREY PUBLISHING
Bloomsbury Publishing Plc
PO Box 883, Oxford, OX1 9PL, UK
29 Earlsfort Terrace, Dublin 2, Ireland
1385 Broadway, 5th Floor, New York, NY 10018, USA
E-mail: info@ospreypublishing.com
www.ospreypublishing.com

OSPREY is a trademark of Osprey Publishing Ltd

First published in Great Britain in 2021

© Osprey Publishing Ltd, 2021

A catalog record for this book is available from the British Library.

ISBN: PB 9781472842817; eBook 9781472842824; ePDF 9781472842794; XML 9781472842800

21 22 23 24 25   10 9 8 7 6 5 4 3 2 1

Maps by Bounford.com
3D BEVs by Paul Kime
Index by Angela Hall
Typeset by PDQ Digital Media Solutions, Bungay, UK
Printed and bound in India by Replika Press Private Ltd.

Artist's note

Readers can find out more about the work of illustrator Jim Laurier via the following website:

www.jimlaurier.com

Osprey Publishing supports the Woodland Trust, the UK's leading woodland conservation charity.

To find out more about our authors and books visit **www.ospreypublishing.com**. Here you will find extracts, author interviews, details of forthcoming events and the option to sign up for our newsletter.

Photographs

All the photographs that appear in this work are US Public Domain.

Japanese names

In this work, Japanese names are presented with the forename first, followed by the family name.

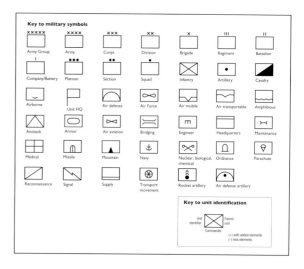

PREVIOUS PAGE: The Japanese battleship *Nagato* in action during the Battle of the Sibuyan Sea.

CONTENTS

INTRODUCTION

For a number of reasons, the Battle of Leyte Gulf has achieved mythical status. Perhaps most obviously, the battle was the largest naval encounter of all time. The United States Navy (USN) brought over 220 combatants (destroyer size and larger) into the battle arrayed in two fleets. One of these was the most powerful naval force on the planet. The Third Fleet included the USN's Fast Carrier Force with 16 fleet and light carriers, and a phalanx of escorts including six of the most powerful battleships in the world. Compared to the Third Fleet, the Seventh Fleet may have lacked striking power, but it was still a significant force with six older battleships and 18 escort carriers assigned to cover the invasion force of 420 amphibious ships carrying 132,400 men bound for the island of Leyte. The Imperial Japanese Navy (IJN) made a supreme effort to turn back the American invasion of the Philippines. This translated into a combined force of some 69 combatants, broken down into four main forces. Among the ships participating were the two Yamato-class battleships (the largest battleships ever built), the IJN's seven other surviving battleships, along with the IJN's 14 remaining heavy cruisers. Most of these heavy ships were concentrated into a single force and given the mission of breaking into Leyte Gulf and destroying the American invasion fleet.

Almost half of TU 77.4.3 ("Taffy 3") is visible in this single image taken from *Kalinin Bay*. In the foreground is *Gambier Bay*; behind her is another escort carrier and two destroyer escorts making smoke.

If only the size of the forces committed to the battle were considered, this would be enough to generate endless fascination. It is also the array of different types of combat that makes the Battle of Leyte Gulf so interesting. Among these are the last battleship duel in history, the first organized kamikaze attacks, three major surface battles, and the heaviest air attacks on ships at sea in naval history. In addition, the battle was extraordinarily complex with four major battles fought in the span of only two days. The interrelated nature of the main encounters made for intense controversy. As the complex and seemingly hopeless Japanese plan unfolded, the USN's Third Fleet was drawn to the north. This opened the door for the IJN's force of battleships and heavy cruisers to charge into Leyte Gulf and gain victory. On the verge of seeming victory, the Japanese inexplicably turned back. The enduring myth that the Japanese were close to victory is the most erroneous among the many myths surrounding the battle.

This is the first of two Osprey Campaign titles covering the battle. In this book, the focus is on the operations of the IJN's First Diversion Attack Force as it made its way to Leyte Gulf. This trek included two major battles – the Battle of the Sibuyan Sea on October 24, 1944 when the Japanese came under concerted air attack from the Third Fleet, and the Battle off Samar the following day, as the still-powerful First Diversion Attack Force headed south toward Leyte Gulf.

ORIGINS OF THE CAMPAIGN

After slow advances in the South Pacific for the second half of 1942 and most of 1943, the growing strength of the USN allowed it to open a second line of advance in the Central Pacific in late 1943. This was the USN's preferred strategy, in no small measure because it was a Navy operation led by Admiral Chester Nimitz, unlike the advance through the South Pacific and New Guinea that was under the strategic direction of Army General Douglas MacArthur. The outline for a two-front offensive against the Japanese was approved at the Trident Conference held in Washington DC on May 12–17, 1943 by the Combined Chiefs of Staff from the United States and the United Kingdom. Landings were conducted in the Gilbert Islands in November 1943 and were followed by the invasion of the Marshalls in January and February 1944. At the Cairo Conference in December 1943, the Allied leaders embraced the advantages of the Central Pacific drive and the benefits of seizing the Mariana Islands in particular. An invasion of the Marianas was scheduled for October 1944.

As the American advance quickened, the debate between Nimitz and MacArthur on its future direction became more heated. At a February and March 1944 planning conference in Washington DC, MacArthur's staff fought for an advance along northern New Guinea into Mindanao in the Philippines. Admiral Ernest King and Nimitz wanted the Central Pacific drive as the primary focus. Nimitz proposed a timetable for the remainder of the year, which was later adopted. It called for the Japanese Central Pacific bastion at Truk to be bypassed, Saipan in the Marianas to be attacked by June 15, and landings on the Palau Islands on October 1. On March 12, 1944, the Joint Chiefs of Staff issued a directive that combined Nimitz's short-term schedule and MacArthur's longer-term goal of invading Mindanao. Truk would be bypassed, allowing the invasion of the Marianas to commence on June 15. Following this, the next targets were the Palaus in mid-September and Mindanao in mid-November.

Both Nimitz's and MacArthur's advances made considerable progress in the first part of 1944. In the Central Pacific, Saipan was invaded on June 15. This prompted the IJN to commit its carrier force for the first time since October 1942 to repel the invasion and defeat the USN in a decisive battle. The result was the Battle of the Philippine Sea, which was the largest carrier battle of the war, and a decisive victory for the USN. The IJN's carrier force was smashed, losing almost 400 aircraft, almost all its trained aviators, and three carriers in the process. Defeat was so comprehensive that the IJN's carrier force would not be ready for the next major American advance in the

The locations of principal USN and IJN forces, October 1944

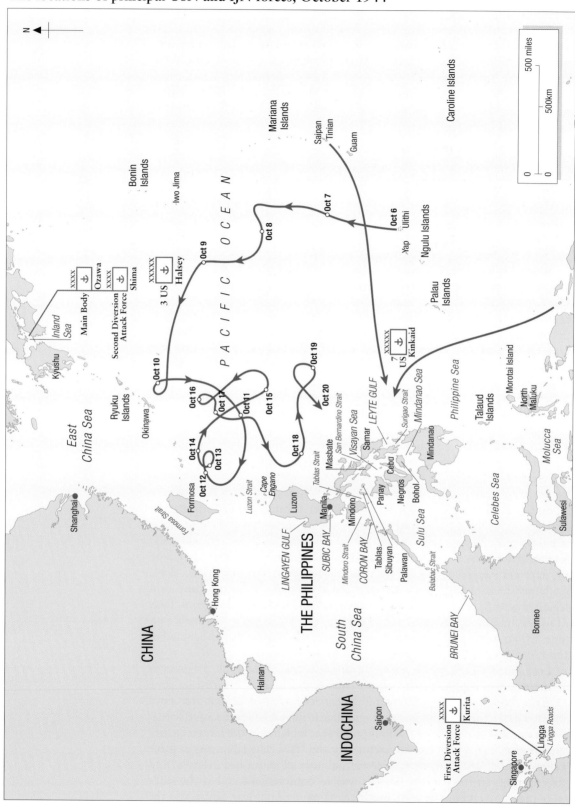

Pacific. The inability of the IJN to reconstitute its carrier force had a massive impact on its planning for the Battle of Leyte Gulf.

The Joint Chief of Staffs' March directive left unclear what the next target would be after Mindanao. The debate over how to combine the two divergent advances now came to a head. MacArthur advocated for a full assault on the Philippines to clear them before the final advance on Japan could begin. King and Nimitz did not believe smashing through the Philippines was wise. They wanted MacArthur to seize Mindanao as an air base to support operations to capture Formosa and a base on the Chinese coast. Once Formosa had been taken, all exports from the resource areas in Southeast Asia to Japan would be cut. The Philippines, King argued, should be bypassed.

Events in China undermined the prospects for King's Formosa–China advance being approved. A major Japanese Army advance in China begun in May 1944 soon made it apparent that Chinese forces would not be able to assist in securing a lodgment on the Chinese coast. Additionally, Formosa was well defended and would require a force of nine divisions to invade. Such a force would be impossible to assemble until mid-1945.

When the Combined Chiefs of Staff met in June 1944, both MacArthur and King refused to budge from their strategic vision. On July 26–27, MacArthur and Nimitz personally presented their plans to President Franklin D. Roosevelt, who was in Hawaii on an inspection tour. This meeting was not going to render a decision (this was a matter for the Joint Chiefs to decide), but even Nimitz later admitted that the Philippines option was more sound. The Joint Chiefs were still unable to express a clear vision of the long-term strategy to defeat Japan, but they did approve MacArthur's plan to invade Leyte on December 20, 1944.

PRELIMINARY OPERATIONS

On August 28, the Third Fleet's carrier force, designated Task Force (TF) 38 under the ultimate command of Admiral William F. Halsey, departed the advanced fleet anchorage at Eniwetok in the Marshalls and headed west. Halsey's orders were to reduce Japanese land-based air power that might interfere with the planned invasions of Morotai off northwestern New Guinea and Peleliu in the Palau Islands. TF 38 proceeded to strike the Palaus on September 6–8 and Mindanao on September 9–10. These raids were unopposed, so Halsey moved on to hit the Visayas in the central Philippines on September 12–13, where American aviators claimed to have destroyed 200 Japanese aircraft in the air or on the ground. Based on this, Halsey assessed that Japanese air power in the region had been neutralized. With this conclusion, he made a momentous recommendation to Nimitz that the preliminary landings on Morotai, Yap, Peleliu, and Mindanao be scrubbed so that the landing on Leyte could be moved up.

Even though this was a dramatic change in plans, it was quickly approved. MacArthur's staff indicated that if the November 15 landing on Mindanao was cancelled, an invasion on Leyte could be mounted on October 20. Nimitz also agreed with the advanced schedule. The request reached the Joint Chiefs of Staff on September 15. After deliberating for a mere 90 minutes, they approved the new plan. The invasion of Leyte was on, and the Japanese were planning another decisive battle to defeat it.

CHRONOLOGY

1944

| October 12–16 | Air battle off Formosa; TF 38 destroys some 500 Japanese aircraft; two USN cruisers are torpedoed but survive. |

October 12–16   Air battle off Formosa; TF 38 destroys some 500 Japanese aircraft; two USN cruisers are torpedoed but survive.

October 17   Japanese spot USN forces on eastern approaches to Leyte Gulf and place *Sho-1* forces on alert.

October 18   0100hrs: Japanese First Diversion Attack Force departs Lingga Roads.

1110hrs: Japanese give the execute order for *Sho-1*.

October 20   US forces land on Leyte.

October 22   First Diversion Attack Force departs Brunei Bay.

October 23   USN submarines ambush First Diversion Attack Force in the Palawan Passage; two heavy cruisers are sunk and one heavily damaged.

October 24   Light carrier *Princeton* sunk by Japanese air attack.

Five USN air attacks hit the First Diversion Attack Force; superbattleship *Musashi* is sunk and heavy cruiser *Myoko* damaged and forced to return.

October 25   0037hrs: First Diversion Attack Force enters the Philippine Sea.

0644hrs: *Yamato* sights Taffy 3.

0659hrs: *Yamato* opens fire on escort carriers.

0703hrs: Kurita orders "General Attack."

0716hrs: Sprague orders the first torpedo attack by escorts.

0727hrs: Heavy cruiser *Kumano* hit by torpedo from *Johnston*.

0735hrs: Heavy cruiser *Suzuya* damaged by air attack and falls out of the engagement.

0740hrs: Kamikazes attack TG 77.4.1 ("Taffy 1").

0742hrs: Sprague orders second torpedo attack by escorts.

0820hrs: Escort carrier *Gambier Bay* crippled by gunfire.

0854hrs: Heavy cruiser *Chikuma* crippled by air attack.

0855hrs: Destroyer *Hoel* sinks.

0900hrs: Range to escort carriers from pursuing Japanese cruisers is down to 8,000 yards.

0905hrs: Heavy cruiser *Chokai* crippled by air attack.

0907hrs: *Gambier Bay* sinks.

0911hrs: Kurita breaks off action.

1005hrs: Destroyer escort *Samuel B. Roberts* sinks.

1010hrs: Destroyer *Johnston* sinks.

1125hrs: Escort carrier *St. Lo* sunk by kamikaze attack.

1315hrs: First air attack by TG 38.1 against First Diversion Attack Force.

1320hrs: Heavy cruiser *Suzuya* sinks.

1500hrs: Last attack by Taffy aircraft against First Diversion Attack Force followed by second attack from TG 38.1.

October 26   Air attacks by TG 38.1 and TG 38.2 cripple *Kumano* and sink light cruiser *Noshiro*.

October 28   First Diversion Attack Force returns to Brunei.

Though the US Navy gained an overwhelming victory, its cost was high. This is a funeral service on *Kalinin Bay* for some of the victims of the Battle off Samar. Taffy 3, which included *Kalinin Bay*, took the brunt of American losses.

9

OPPOSING COMMANDERS

UNITED STATES NAVY

There were two primary commands involved in the Leyte invasion. The ground forces, most supporting air forces, and the Seventh Fleet were under command of General Douglas MacArthur in his capacity as Supreme Commander Southwest Pacific Area. Halsey's Third Fleet did not answer to MacArthur, but instead to Admiral Chester W. Nimitz who was Commander-in-Chief Pacific Fleet and Pacific Ocean Areas. MacArthur ordered that the Seventh Fleet not communicate with the Third Fleet directly. This bifurcated chain of command was an obvious flaw in the command structure, and this flaw was fully exposed during the battle.

Overall direction of USN naval strategy and resource allocation worldwide was under the charge of **Admiral Ernest J. King** in his dual capacities as Commander-in-Chief, US Fleet and Chief of Naval Operations. King was a hard-charging leader who aggressively sought to fight the war in the Pacific as seen fit by the Navy and to keep what he saw as Army interference to a minimum. **Admiral Chester W. Nimitz** retained strategic control of the Third Fleet during the battle. Since taking over the Pacific Fleet after the Pearl Harbor debacle, Nimitz had proved himself to be an outstanding leader and strategist. Nimitz was well regarded by his subordinates because he tried not to meddle and let them get on with the tasks he had given them. However, he kept close watch of his subordinates during major operations.

A key command figure in this battle, and probably the person most responsible for how the battle unfolded, was **Admiral William F. Halsey**. His role was controversial since he commanded the most powerful

In this scene from November 30, 1944, Vice Admiral John S. McCain, Sr is decorated with the Navy Cross by Admiral William F. Halsey aboard McCain's flagship *Hancock*. Halsey commanded the Third Fleet at the Battle of Leyte Gulf and McCain was one of his carrier task force commanders and later took command of TF 38.

force in the battle and did so with the extreme aggression he was noted for. After graduation from the US Naval Academy in 1904, Halsey spent most of his early career on torpedo boats and destroyers. In 1934, the then Chief of the Bureau of Aeronautics, Ernest King, offered him command of carrier *Saratoga*. Since by law carrier commanders had to be qualified naval aviators, Halsey attended a 12-week aviation course for senior commanders and earned his aviator's wings on May 15, 1935 at the age of 52. He was the senior carrier division commander in the USN at the start of the war. Halsey achieved legendary status early in the war when he led his carriers on several raids against the Japanese, including the Raid on Tokyo in April 1942. A skin disease made Halsey miss Midway, but after recovering he was sent to change the trajectory of the precarious Guadalcanal campaign. He did so but was rashly aggressive in the process. His willingness to fight the Japanese at every turn with whatever he had paid off with victory at Guadalcanal. Halsey directed naval operations as the USN fought up the Solomons in 1943. In another bold operation, he sent two carriers with only land-based air cover to attack a large force of Japanese heavy cruisers in Rabaul. Again, his boldness paid off: the risky operation saved the American beachhead on Bougainville Island from attack.

Vice Admiral Thomas C. Kinkaid (left center) pictured with General Douglas MacArthur (center) on the flag bridge of light cruiser *Phoenix* during the pre-invasion bombardment of Los Negros Island on February 28, 1944. Kinkaid proved adept working with the US Army and even learned how to handle MacArthur.

In May 1944, Halsey was given command of the Third Fleet. He witnessed what he thought was the incomplete USN victory at the Philippine Sea and criticized Vice Admiral Raymond A. Spruance for his caution that allowed the IJN's carrier force to escape complete destruction. This view was shared by many other American naval officers. When the Third Fleet encountered the IJN's remaining strength at Leyte Gulf, the stage was set for Halsey's most controversial decision of the war.

Vice Admiral Marc Mitscher was the commander of TF 38, the Third Fleet's fast carrier force. Mitscher was one of the pioneers of USN aviation and had considerable experience as a carrier skipper and a carrier task force commander. He had just led TF 58 (the designation of the fast carrier task force when it was under command of the Fifth Fleet) at the invasion of the Marshalls, the neutralization of Truk, and the Battle of the Philippine Sea. Nobody was more familiar with large carrier operations than Mitscher. His relationship with Halsey was not good. When Halsey assumed tactical command of TF 38, which happened often, Mitscher would give recommendations to Halsey but sulked when they were not taken. Task Force 38 was divided into four subordinate task groups. These were commanded by a quartet of highly experienced, capable, and aggressive officers. Task Group (TG) 38.1 was under the command of **Vice Admiral John S. McCain;**

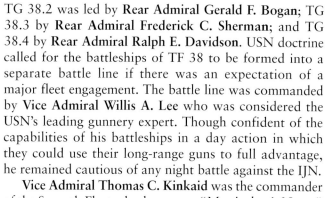

TG 38.2 was led by **Rear Admiral Gerald F. Bogan**; TG 38.3 by **Rear Admiral Frederick C. Sherman**; and TG 38.4 by **Rear Admiral Ralph E. Davidson**. USN doctrine called for the battleships of TF 38 to be formed into a separate battle line if there was an expectation of a major fleet engagement. The battle line was commanded by **Vice Admiral Willis A. Lee** who was considered the USN's leading gunnery expert. Though confident of the capabilities of his battleships in a day action in which they could use their long-range guns to full advantage, he remained cautious of any night battle against the IJN.

Vice Admiral Thomas C. Kinkaid was the commander of the Seventh Fleet, also known as "MacArthur's Navy." Kinkaid's background was in the surface navy, and he was in command of a cruiser division right after the war began. He saw action at Coral Sea and Midway and was given command of a carrier task force during the Guadalcanal campaign. He did not perform well in this capacity; of note, he was the last surface admiral to command a carrier task force in combat during the war. He was not given another carrier command, but did redeem himself. In January 1943, Kinkaid became Commander of the North Pacific Force and was ordered to get along with his US Army counterparts. Kinkaid led the recapture of Attu and Kiska in the Aleutians and demonstrated an ability to work with the Army. This success presented him with a job dreaded by any self-respecting naval officer—working for Douglas MacArthur. As Commander, Allied Naval Forces Southwest Pacific Area and Commander of the Seventh Fleet, Kinkaid conducted a string of successful amphibious operations on New Guinea and demonstrated an ability to please the prickly MacArthur.

The Seventh Fleet was a large organization comprised of the Northern and Southern Attack forces for the two invasion points on Leyte. The part of the Seventh Fleet involved with the battles detailed in this volume was TG 77.4, the Escort Carrier Group. This was under command of Rear Admiral Thomas L. Sprague who was also in direct command of one of the task groups (77.4.1) designated as "Taffy 1." Sprague was an experienced aviator who had commanded fleet carrier *Intrepid* before taking over a division of escort carriers prior to the invasion of the Marianas. "Taffy 2" (77.4.2) was under the command of Rear Admiral Felix B. Stump. He was also an experienced aviator who had commanded fleet carrier *Lexington* before gaining flag rank and assuming command of a division of escort carriers. "Taffy 3" (77.4.3) was led by Rear Admiral Clifton A.F. Sprague. Sprague gave an epic performance at Leyte Gulf. He was an experienced aviator who had commanded fleet carrier *Wasp* before assuming command of an escort carrier division in July.

IMPERIAL JAPANESE NAVY

Imperial General Headquarters directed the strategic operations of the Imperial Army and Navy. The Naval General Staff, which doubled as the navy section of the Imperial General Headquarters, was responsible for strategic and operational planning for the IJN. The Naval General Staff provided strategic direction to the Combined Fleet, which was the IJN's offensive force. Since May 1944, **Admiral Soemu Toyoda** was in command of the Combined Fleet. He was an experienced and intelligent officer who had been among those opposed to going to war with the US. Toyoda was a potential successor to Admiral Isoroku Yamamoto as Combined Fleet commander after Yamamoto's death in April 1943. Instead, Admiral Mineichi Koga got the job. After Koga's death in March 1944, it was Toyoda's turn to try to reverse the IJN's declining fortunes. He assumed command of the Combined Fleet on May 3, 1944 and oversaw the defeat at Philippine Sea the next month. This decisive defeat left him few options to defend the Philippines. The plan he developed was fatally flawed for several reasons, as will be detailed later.

The Combined Fleet's principal units comprised the Mobile Force under the command of **Vice Admiral Jisaburo Ozawa**. At Leyte Gulf he was in direct command of the Main Body that was composed of the IJN's remaining carriers.

The First Diversion Attack Force was part of the Mobile Force but proceeded independently from Ozawa's force. It was comprised of the majority of the IJN's remaining battleships and heavy cruisers. As such, it was the IJN's principal striking force and its commander, **Vice Admiral Takeo Kurita**, was the IJN's principal and easily most controversial command figure of the battle. Kurita had seen extensive action during the war and was no stranger to tough fights. At the start of the war, he was in command of a division of four heavy cruisers. His command supported the invasion of Java in 1942, where it finished off the USN heavy cruiser *Houston* and then took part in the successful raid into the Indian Ocean in April 1942. In June 1942, he suffered defeat for the first time when USN aircraft sank one of his cruisers and heavily damaged another at the Battle of Midway. In July 1942, Kurita assumed command of a battleship division of two Kongo-class battleships. On the night of October 13, his battleships conducted the most successful action by any IJN battleship during the entire war when they executed a devastating bombardment of Henderson Field on Guadalcanal that temporarily neutralized the airfield.

Admiral Soemu Toyoda was the author of *Sho-1*, the IJN's defense of the Philippines. The plan he devised was more of a vehicle for the IJN's self-immolation than one with any prospect for success. This is Toyoda aboard his flagship, light cruiser *Oyodo*, in about September 1944.

Vice Admiral Takeo Kurita was the pivotal IJN leader during the Battle of Leyte Gulf. Charged with executing a plan with no hope of success, he declined to lead his entire force to its total destruction.

Kurita's next command was the Second Fleet that was composed of the IJN's battleships and heavy cruisers. Before the Battle of the Philippine Sea, the Second Fleet was subsumed into the Mobile Force as support elements for the carriers. Kurita commanded one of the Mobile Force's carrier task groups at the Battle of the Philippine Sea. When the battleships and heavy cruisers were stripped from the carriers and sent to the Singapore area, Kurita took command of this force, now designated the First Diversion Attack Force, and assumed his fateful role in the battle.

Kurita split his two slowest battleships from his direct command and placed these under **Vice Admiral Shoji Nishimura**. This force was designated the First Diversion Attack Force's Third Section. Also active in the battle was the Southwest Area Force under **Vice Admiral Gunichi Mikawa**. **Vice Admiral Kiyohide Shima** led the Second Diversion Attack Force that was under Mikawa's command, even though it was operating in the same area and had the same objective as Kurita's force. Also under the command of the Southwest Area Force was the First Air Fleet under Vice Admiral Takijiro Onishi and the Second Air Fleet commanded by Vice Admiral Shigeru Fukudome. Onishi was one of the IJN's principal air power advocates. He was known for his aggressive nature as evidenced during the battle when he initiated planned suicide attacks.

Vice Admiral Shigeru Fukudome (seated, left) pictured with his family, probably in 1945. From the start of the war until March 1944, Fukudome was the Chief of Staff of the Combined Fleet. On March 31, 1944, his aircraft crashed in a storm and he became the first IJN flag officer to be captured by the enemy. Later released by Filipino guerrillas, he was commander of the Second Air Fleet at the start of the Battle of Leyte Gulf even though he possessed no prior experience with naval aviation.

OPPOSING FORCES

By October 1944, the course of the Pacific War had turned sharply against Japan. The IJN had taken severe losses in the first three years of the conflict but had retained the core of its battleship and heavy cruiser fleets. Toyoda allocated almost every remaining major combatant to take part in the defense of the Philippines. In contrast to the IJN, whose strength had dwindled throughout the war, the USN had grown exponentially in size and power since December 1941. The forces employed in the invasion of Leyte dwarfed those of the IJN. From Table 1 below, it is obvious that the Japanese stood little chance of gaining anything that looked like victory.

Table 1: Total forces employed at Leyte Gulf

	IJN	USN
Airpower		
Fleet carriers	1	8
Light carriers	3	8
Escort carriers	0	18
Total carrier aircraft	116	1,500
Land-based aircraft	Approx. 350 operational on October 24	0
Surface combatants		
Battleships	9	12
Heavy cruisers	14	13
Light cruisers	7	15
Destroyers	35	147
Destroyer escorts	0	14
Total Combatants	69	235

Since this volume covers the air–sea Battle of the Sibuyan Sea and the Battle off Samar, only those forces engaged in those actions will be examined.

UNITED STATES NAVY

Task Force 38

Simply stated, TF 38 was the most powerful naval formation in the world in October 1944. It alone possessed considerably more firepower than the entire IJN. As had became standard practice, TF 38 was broken down into

four task groups. A task group was usually assigned between one and three fleet carriers and two light carriers. Each task group had an escort force of up to two battleships, two to four cruisers, and a variable number of destroyers (nine to 21 in October 1944). The battleships were pulled from the carrier screen and formed into a battle line with a cruiser and destroyer escort whenever there was the prospect of a major fleet engagement with the IJN. The striking power of TF 38 was diminished during the battle since TG 38.1 had been sent to the fleet anchorage at Ulithi to replenish and was unable to take part in the strikes on October 24.

The backbone of the Third Fleet was its force of fleet carriers, almost all Essex-class ships. In this view, *Intrepid* is photographed from the rear seat of a Helldiver dive-bomber after taking off to attack the Japanese force in the Battle of the Sibuyan Sea on October 24, 1944. *Intrepid*'s air group launched three major attacks during the day.

Fleet carriers

TF 38 possessed eight fleet carriers during the battle. All but one of these were Essex-class ships with the last being the unsinkable *Enterprise*. Arrival of the Essex class, beginning in August 1943, transformed the striking power and capabilities of the Fast Carrier Force. At 37,000 tons full load, Essex-class carriers were the most powerful ships of the war. Their excellent design balanced striking power, speed and endurance, and defensive capabilities. Since their principal design focus was handling a large air group, they were excellent offensive platforms and could embark as many as 100 aircraft. This offensive punch was combined with a top speed of 33 knots, range of over 15,000NM, and a heavy antiaircraft battery of 12 5in./38 guns and as many as 72 40mm and 58 20mm guns. The veteran *Enterprise* was slightly smaller and less capable than the Essex-class ships, but still carried an air group of some 90 aircraft.

In addition to the fleet carriers, TF 38 operated eight Independence-class light carriers. These useful ships were the result of a crash conversion program from the hulls of Cleveland-class light cruisers. At just over 15,000

Light carrier *Cowpens* photographed on August 31, 1944 en route to strike the Palaus. The second light carrier in the distance is *Independence*. The light carrier air groups were comprised mostly of fighters; their main mission was usually fleet air defense to allow the Essex-class air groups to focus on offensive operations.

tons full load displacement, they were large enough to embark an air group of 34 aircraft on a fast, well-protected hull.

Carrier air groups and aircraft

In early 1944, an Essex-class air group was comprised of a 36-aircraft fighter squadron, a 36-aircraft dive-bomber squadron, and a torpedo squadron with 18 aircraft. On July 31, 1944, authorization was given to reduce the dive-bomber squadron from 36 to 24 aircraft and increase the size of the fighter squadron up to 54 aircraft. The fighter squadron also included a detachment of four radar-equipped night-fighters and usually some photo-reconnaissance Hellcats. The torpedo squadron was unaltered. Before the Battle of Leyte Gulf, Essex-class air groups were in the process of this transition. Each light carrier embarked an air group of 25 fighters and nine torpedo planes.

Under normal operational conditions, the search range of USN carrier aircraft was about 325NM. This was attained by carrying extra fuel instead of ordnance. The limited strike range of carrier air groups imposed a real limitation on operations. Actual range was dependent on several tactical conditions but was usually about 200NM.

The arrival of the new Essex-class carriers was accompanied by the arrival of new aircraft to operate off their decks. At Leyte Gulf, the standard USN carrier fighter was the Grumman F6F-3 Hellcat. Entering combat service in late 1943, the Hellcat was far superior to its Japanese counterpart, the Mitsubishi A6M "Zero" fighter. The American fighter possessed advantages in protection, speed, and firepower by virtue of its tough and armored airframe, armament of six .50-cal. machine guns, and its powerful Pratt & Whitney R-2800 engine. The only advantage left to the Zero was its maneuverability; as a consequence, Hellcat pilots were trained to avoid dogfights with the Zero.

An F6F Hellcat taking off from *Lexington* on October 12, 1944 to conduct an attack on Japanese facilities on Formosa. By this point of the war, the Hellcat had gained total supremacy against Japanese aircraft. This allowed TF 38 to successfully conduct strikes against Japanese-held islands, even those with large concentrations of aircraft.

Dive-bomber squadrons used the Curtiss SB2C Helldiver. This aircraft replaced the well-loved Douglas SBD Dauntless after the Battle of the Philippine Sea. After sorting out the aircraft's many problems during an excessively long gestation period, the SB2C-3 version with its larger engine and other modifications was approved for fleet service. The aircraft was fast (top speed of almost 300mph), rugged, and could carry a bombload of 1,000lb. However, even 1,000lb bombs were unable to sink large, heavily protected battleships.

The USN's standard torpedo bomber since the latter part of 1942 was the Grumman TBF/TBM Avenger. It was the best carrier torpedo aircraft of the war and was embarked on fleet, light, and escort carriers because of its versatility. The Avenger was reliable in service, able to withstand battle damage, and was able to perform as a torpedo plane or a conventional bomber. However, to be effective, a torpedo bomber needed a reliable torpedo. Since 1938 the standard USN air-launched torpedo was the Mark 13. During the first part of the war, the Mark 13 was chronically unreliable, and these problems took two years to completely rectify. By 1944, the Avenger finally had a functioning torpedo that it could drop at 270mph and at a more survivable altitude of up to 800ft. The Mark 13, with its 600lb warhead, was essential if the American carrier air groups hoped to sink battleships.

USN ship attack tactics

After problems earlier in the war with fragmented strikes and a faulty torpedo, by 1944 USN carrier air groups had a well-rehearsed and proven doctrine for attacking Japanese naval targets. The goal was to mount a coordinated attack with fighters, dive-bombers, and torpedo planes to overwhelm the target's defenses. Each carrier air group conducted its attack separately. A lack of an overall coordinator sometimes resulted in over-concentration on a single target.

In a coordinated attack, the Helldivers attacked first. The standard dive-bombing profile began with a shallow approach from 20,000ft followed

SB2C Helldivers loading drop tanks on board *Lexington* on October 25, 1944. After a long and painful gestation period, the Helldiver proved itself a very capable dive-bomber that eventually sank more Japanese ships than any other type of Allied aircraft.

Flight-deck crews prepare to load a Mark 13 torpedo on a TBM Avenger on board *Wasp* on October 13, 1944. Note the plywood stabilizer on the torpedo's fins and drag ring on its nose that allowed the torpedo to be dropped from higher altitudes and corrected some of its erratic behavior after entering the water. Avengers were a staple in the air groups of fleet, light, and escort carriers.

by a steep dive from between 15,000 and 12,000ft. To present as large a target as possible, the target ship was attacked along its longitudinal axis. This explained the typical Japanese evasion tactic of steering a complete circle since it gave the dive-bomber pilots a constantly changing target axis. Helldivers dove at 65–70° and dropped their 1,000lb bomb at 1,500–2,000ft above the target. To attack from different directions, the Helldiver squadron was divided into divisions of six aircraft. Ideally, as the dive-bombers were attacking, the Avengers commenced their torpedo runs. The preferred tactic was an "anvil" attack that called for Avengers to approach the target simultaneously from both bows making it difficult for the target to maneuver without exposing itself to attack.

USN *antiaircraft defenses*

By October 1944, USN fleet air defense had reached a high level of proficiency. This, combined with the growing inexperience of Japanese aviators, provided a large degree of immunity from conventional Japanese air attacks. The bedrocks of fleet air defense were early radar detection, an effective combat air patrol (CAP), and well-directed antiaircraft fire.

The standard air warning radar installed on large ships was the SK radar that could regularly detect formations of enemy aircraft flying at high altitudes out to 100NM. The SM radar fitted aboard carriers provided height information that was critical for effective combat air patrol (CAP) operations. The most effective method of defeating Japanese air attacks was placing Hellcats between the task force and the incoming strike. Fighter direction was difficult for many reasons, but by 1944 USN fighter direction was based on a solid doctrine, and intercepts of enemy aircraft well before they reached the task force was routine. The inner layer of air defense was provided by ships' antiaircraft fire. USN task groups deployed in a circular formation in the face of air attack with the carriers deployed in the center. The outer zone of antiaircraft protection was provided by the radar-controlled 5in./38 gun that was effective out to 10,000 yards. Intermediate protection was provided by the 40mm Bofors gun fitted in either dual or quad mounts. The Bofors was also director-controlled and effective out to about 3,000 yards. Last-ditch protection was the job of the 20mm Oerlikon gun fitted in single mounts. When fitted with the Mark 14 gyro-sight, the 20mm was effective out to about 1,500 yards.

Surface combatants

In addition to its formidable line-up of 16 carriers, TF 38 also possessed a powerful array of surface combatants totaling six battleships, five heavy cruisers, seven light cruisers, and as many as 63 destroyers. The USN did not see its battleships being limited to providing antiaircraft support to the carriers. An important part of TF 38's battle plan was to give the battleships a chance to engage the IJN's battle fleet, and failing that, to finish off any crippled vessels created by USN carrier strikes.

The battle line was comprised of six battleships, all commissioned after 1941. All carried 16in. naval guns and the best fire-control systems in existence. They were also extremely well protected against both air and surface attack. *Washington* was a North Carolina-class ship mounting nine 16in./45 guns and 20 5in./38 dual-purpose guns. Her top speed was 28 knots. *Alabama*, *Massachusetts*, and *South Dakota* were three of the four ships of the South Dakota class. They also carried nine 16in./45 guns but possessed a slightly slower top speed. They were, however, better protected than the preceding North Carolina class. *Iowa* and *New Jersey* were the first two ships of the Iowa class and were the only class of USN battleships built without restrictions from the prewar system of naval treaties. At over 57,000 tons full load, they were big enough to carry heavy protection, nine 16in./50 main battery guns, and machinery to propel the ship at 33 knots. Except for the two Japanese Yamato-class battleships, all modern USN battleships were better protected and better armed than any Japanese battleship. In addition to this, USN battleships had the immense advantage of superior fire-control systems. The USN augmented its optical rangefinders with radar,

Baltimore-class heavy cruiser *Canberra* is shown operating with TF 38 on October 10, 1944 just before the air battle off Formosa. Three days later, *Canberra* was torpedoed and heavily damaged, but was salvaged and returned to service.

which served as quicker and more accurate rangefinders. The Mark 8 radar, introduced in 1943, was capable of blind fire (important in night combat), and could track a battleship-sized target at 40,000 yards and a smaller target at up to 31,000 yards.

TF 38 heavy cruisers came in two types: the Treaty cruisers built before the war, and the wartime construction of the Baltimore class. The USN light cruisers assigned to TF 38 were a mix of Atlanta-class ships best suited to an antiaircraft role, and the 10,000-ton Cleveland class that carried a formidable main battery of 12 6in. guns with a high rate of fire. By October 1944, the standard USN fleet destroyer was the Fletcher class. These were balanced ships with high speed and a main battery of five 5in./38 guns and ten torpedo tubes. The standard destroyer torpedo was the Mark 15, which also had a series of early-war issues. These problems had been addressed by late 1943; using radar to fire its torpedoes, American destroyers proved themselves to be very capable surface warfare ships.

Fletcher-class destroyers were the most successful of any USN destroyers during the war. A total of 175 of these well-balanced ships entered service. This is *Hoel*, photographed on August 10, 1944.

The escort carrier group

The invasion of Leyte included the largest concentration of escort carriers yet seen in the war. A maximum of 18 were used to provide air defense to the Seventh Fleet and close air support to the troops ashore. The Sangamon class was converted from oilers and had a full load displacement of almost 24,000 tons. Four were available. The balance of the escort carrier force was comprised of Casablanca-class ships. These were mass-produced conversions from merchant hulls.

Because of their low speed, inadequate armament, and small air groups, escort carriers operated in groups. For the Leyte operation, three groups of six escort carriers were formed. Sangamon-class ships were large enough to carry two aircraft squadrons. In October 1944, this included a fighter squadron with up to 22 Hellcats (one carrier retained a fighter squadron of 24 older FM-2 Wildcat fighters) and a squadron of nine Avengers. The

Escort carrier *Gambier Bay* photographed in April 1944. She was one of 50 Casablanca-class escort carriers mass produced in the period of only one year. All these ships were slow, unprotected, and weakly armed. The ship's only 5in. gun can be seen on her stern. Escort carriers were entirely unsuited for a clash with IJN surface units.

smaller Casablanca-class carriers embarked a composite air group with a mix of up to 16 Wildcats and 12 Avengers. This number fluctuated depending on operational and combat losses and the availability of replacement aircraft. Though escort carrier air groups were not highly proficient in a maritime attack role, they still trained for this mission and had the aircraft and weapons to execute it.

Table 2: Characteristics of escort carrier group warships

Ship	Tonnage (full load)	Weapons	Armor	Top speed
Sangamon-class escort carriers	23,875	Two x 5in./38, 18 x 40mm, 19 x 20mm	None	18 knots
Casablanca-class escort carriers	10,900	One x 5in./38, 16 x 40mm, 20 x 20mm	None	19 knots
Fletcher-class destroyers	2,500	Five x 5in./38, ten x 40mm, seven x 20mm, ten x 21in. torpedo tubes	None	37 knots
Butler-class destroyer escort	1,773	Two x 5in./38, four x 40mm, ten x 20mm, three x 21in. torpedo tubes	None	24 knots

Submarines

Both the Pacific Fleet and the Seventh Fleet deployed submarines to support the invasion. USN submarines were crippled early in the war by their deficient Mark 14 torpedo, but by 1944 this had been rectified. By this point in the war, the standard USN fleet submarines were the Gato and the Balao classes. These were excellent boats with a long range and an excellent radar suite, and embarked up to 24 torpedoes. Most importantly, they were commanded by a very aggressive corps of skippers who had learned how to attack Japanese convoys and even fleet units with a high probability of success. Their effectiveness was multiplied by ineffective IJN antisubmarine warfare tactics and weaponry.

Logistical support

TF 38 had its own extensive fleet train that allowed it to stay at sea for prolonged periods if necessary. This large collection of ships was designated TG 30.8. Indicating the size of the effort devoted to at-sea logistics was the fact that 33 oilers were assigned to TG 30.8, along with ammunition ships and fleet tugs. To keep the carriers stocked with aircraft, 11 escort carriers were also present carrying replacement aircraft. Though the Japanese never made any attempt to attack the fleet train, it was well defended by 17 destroyers and 26 destroyer escorts. Periodically, each carrier task group rotated off the line and went to Ulithi for full replenishment and crew recreation.

IMPERIAL JAPANESE NAVY

The First Diversion Attack Force was the centerpiece of the Japanese plan at Leyte Gulf and will be examined in detail. Because they took part in the air battles of October 24, land-based IJN air forces will also be reviewed.

The First Diversion Attack Force

After the destruction of the IJN's carrier force at the Battle of the Philippine Sea, the principal striking power of the IJN resided in its large force of battleships and heavy cruisers. For the all-out effort to defend the Philippines, these were concentrated into a single operational entity. The resulting formation was named the First Diversion Attack Force and placed under the command of Vice Admiral Kurita. With five battleships, ten heavy cruisers, two light cruisers, and 15 destroyers, it was the largest surface force yet assembled by the Japanese for a single mission and among the largest such concentrations of the entire war.

After its arrival at Lingga Roads near Singapore on July 22, Kurita drilled his force relentlessly. The primary exercise was storming an anchorage with the First Diversion Attack Force divided into two parts, each led by *Yamato* or *Musashi*. As usual, the emphasis was given to night-fighting. Antiaircraft combat was another point of emphasis since the fleet would have to operate without air cover. The fitting of radar on every ship gave the Japanese renewed confidence and great efforts were made to incorporate radar into gunnery drills.

The heart of *Sho-1* was the impressive collection of battleships and heavy cruisers designated to the First Diversion Attack Force. Several of those are in this photograph taken at Brunei before they departed for Leyte Gulf. From left to right are battleships *Musashi*, *Yamato*, a cruiser, and battleship *Nagato*.

Battleships

In keeping with its mission to deliver the decisive blow, the First Diversion Attack Force was allocated the most powerful of the IJN's remaining battleships. The force was built around the superbattleships *Yamato* and *Musashi*, which had yet to fire their main guns in anger. The two Yamato-class ships were designed with the highest levels of firepower (in the form of 18.1in. main guns) and protection possible to give them a qualitative edge over any USN battleships. However, their 18.1in. guns possessed only a small range advantage over the USN's 16in. battleship guns and used inferior fire-control equipment. Also present was *Nagato*, laid down in 1917 but modernized between 1934 and 1936; the ship carried 16in. guns but was relatively slow with a maximum speed of 25 knots. *Kongo* and *Haruna* were both originally launched in 1913 and 1915, respectively, as battlecruisers before being modernized twice between 1927 and 1936. These ships carried 14in. main guns and even after modernization were not as well protected compared to USN battleships, but were faster at 30 knots.

Table 3: Characteristics of the First Diversion Task Force's warships

Ship	Tonnage (full load)	Weapons	Armor	Top speed
Battleships				
Yamato, Musashi	73,000	Nine x 18.1in. guns, six x 6.1in. guns, 24 x 5in. guns (*Musashi* x 12), 152 x 25mm (*Musashi* x 130)	Main belt 16in., horizontal 7.9–9.1in.	27.5 knots
Nagato	46,356	Eight x 16in./45, 18 x 5.5in./50, eight x 5in./40, 96 x 25mm	Main belt 12in., horizontal 8.1in.	25 knots
Kongo, Haruna	36,601	Eight x 14in./45, 12 x 6in./50, eight x 5in./40, 122 x 25mm	Main belt 8in., horizontal 4.75in.	30.5 knots
Heavy cruisers				
Haguro, Myoko	15,933	Ten x 8in./50, eight x 5in./40, 52 x 25mm, 16 x 24in. torpedo tubes	Main belt 4in., horizontal 3in.	33 knots
Atago, Chokai, Maya, Takao	15,641	Ten x 8in./50 (*Maya* x eight), eight x 5in./40 (*Maya* x 12), 38–66 x 25mm, 16 x 24in. torpedo tubes	Main belt 4in., horizontal 3in.	35.5 knots
Kumano, Suzuya	15,057	Ten x 8in./50, eight x 5in./40, 50–56 x 25mm, 12 x 24in. torpedo tubes	Main belt 3.9in., horizontal 2.95in.	35 knots
Chikuma, Tone	15,239	Eight x 8in./50, eight x 5in./40, 45–57 x 25mm, 12 x 24in. torpedo tubes	Main belt 5.7in., horizontal 4.76in.	35 knots
Light cruisers				
Noshiro, Yahagi	8,534	Six x 6in./50, four x 3.15in., 32 x 25mm, eight x 24in. torpedo tubes	Main belt 2.36in., horizontal 0.78in.	35 knots
Destroyers				
Kagero class (5)	2,540	Four x 5in./50, 21–28 x 25mm, eight x 24in. torpedo tubes	None	35 knots
Yugumo class (9)	2,520	Six x 5in./50, 26 x 25mm, eight x 24in. torpedo tubes	None	35 knots
Shimakaze	3,300	Six x 5in./50, 21 x 25mm, 15 x 24in. torpedo tubes	None	39 knots

Other surface combatants

Among the 32 warships of the First Diversion Attack Force were ten heavy cruisers. Since it withheld most of its battleships for decisive battles, the IJN's heavy cruisers had been very active during the war and had performed

Musashi departed Brunei Bay on the morning of October 22; the following day she was exposed to relentless air attack and became the largest ship ever sunk by aircraft up to that point.

well. These ships were fast, heavily armed, and crewed by well-trained men. Unlike USN heavy cruisers, IJN heavy cruisers mounted a heavy torpedo battery of between 12 and 16 torpedo tubes. The principal IJN torpedo was the incomparable Type 93 with a maximum range of 43,746 yards carrying a 1,082lb warhead. Japanese heavy cruisers carried reloads for their torpedo tubes. All had received massive augmentation to their antiaircraft batteries during the war. The two modern light cruisers were designed as destroyer leaders and were not as heavily armed or protected as USN light cruisers. By this point of the war, the IJN's destroyer force had taken extremely heavy losses. Only 15 were available for the First Diversion Attack Force, which was inadequate to screen 17 major warships. The IJN's destroyers had performed brilliantly in many night actions during the war using their Type 93s with deadly precision. Though IJN destroyers were excellent torpedo boats, they possessed indifferent capabilities as antisubmarine and antiaircraft warfare platforms.

IJN antiaircraft capabilities

No force in naval history was subjected to a greater scale of air attack than the First Diversion Attack Force. During the span of three days (October 24–26), some 1,000 USN sorties were conducted against Kurita's force. Since the First Diversion Attack Force had been split from the carriers of the Main Body, and the IJN's land-based air forces were too weak to provide air cover, the First Diversion Attack Force was very much on its own to defend against air attack on its trek to Leyte Gulf. To defend its surface fleet, the IJN fitted a steadily rising number of antiaircraft guns on its combatants. The most common gun was the Type 96 25mm single and triple mount. *Yamato* and *Musashi* led the way with 152 and 130, respectively; heavy cruisers carried up to 66, and destroyers up to 28. Unfortunately for the IJN, the Type 96 25mm gun was a mediocre weapon in every respect. Even the Japanese recognized that the Type 96, with its inadequate training and elevation speeds, low sustained rate of fire, and excessive blast which affected accuracy, prevented it from providing protection from American air attack. In particular, the single mount was almost worthless since it had only an open-ring sight for fire control, could not cope with high-speed targets, and

Of the 18 prewar IJN heavy cruisers, 14 still existed by October 1944. Ten of these were allocated to the First Diversion Attack Force, making it the largest concentration of IJN heavy cruisers during the entire war. Of the ten, only two were not heavily damaged or sunk. One of these two, *Haguro*, is shown here in April 1936.

was difficult to handle. Even when the Type 96 hit its target, its small shell often failed to do real damage to the robust Helldivers and Avengers.

Augmenting the Type 96 was the Type 89 5in. high-angle gun adopted in February 1932. This weapon was well liked since it was reliable, possessed high elevating speeds, a high muzzle velocity, and fired a large shell. Though the gun was decent, its fire-control system was inferior. It was unable to track high-speed targets and took some 20 seconds to track slower targets and then another 10–12 seconds to produce a fire-control solution; often, the fire-control solutions were inaccurate. The inadequacies of the Type 96 25mm and the Type 89 5in. guns meant Japanese ships were vulnerable to air attack.

Logistical support

By October 1944, the IJN suffered from a lack of strategic mobility. This was due to a lack of fuel oil and a lack of oilers to carry it. The problem was deeper since the IJN's ability to conduct replenishment at sea had reached a low point before the battle. From May to September, the IJN lost 18 tankers, making the lack of fuel in the forward areas even more pressing. This problem was partially addressed when the First Diversion Attack Force was moved to Lingga Roads, which was close to fuel sources on Borneo and Sumatra. The IJN also lifted the requirement that all fuel had to be processed. This allowed light oil from Tarakan on Borneo to be burned in ships' boilers without refining. The downside to this was that it possessed a heavy sulfur content that could damage boilers and was highly volatile.

Fueling his ships was one of Kurita's primary concerns. Because fuel would be used at an alarming rate once battle was joined, his force would have to refuel, particularly the destroyers, immediately before and after the decisive battle. Because the IJN lacked practice in refueling underway, this had to be done in a protected bay. To support Kurita's force, the Japanese assembled a force of eight tankers. Several were sent to Brunei Bay in northwestern Borneo to top the fleet off before battle and to service it when it returned. Even with this, Kurita's force would have limited fuel for extended high-speed operations. This was driven by the destroyers' range of some 5,000NM steaming at 18 knots. Since it was 1,400NM from Brunei to Leyte Gulf using the San Bernardino Strait, and the force would have to maneuver under air attack and then use high speeds in any surface engagement, the fleet could not proceed further than to Leyte and directly back. The fuel state of the destroyers on October 26 was indicative of the perilous state of IJN logistics. Many were down to only a few tons of fuel and barely made it to Coron Bay in the Calamian Islands, where a tanker was waiting.

Had, against all odds, the First Diversion Attack Force achieved its objective and returned to Lingga, it would have taken some time to refuel and rearm the fleet and prepare it for another major operation. While the USN could maintain a huge invasion fleet on station for an extended period, the IJN had been essentially reduced to a raiding force capable of only sporadic operations.

Land-based air forces

Key to the entire Japanese plan was control of the air. With the IJN's carrier force reduced to impotence, the burden of striking USN forces and providing cover for the First Diversion Attack Force was thrust upon the IJN's land-based air forces. Though there were two air fleets assigned to the Philippines by the start of the battle, they could render little support. The First Air Fleet was headquartered in Manila under the command of Vice Admiral Onishi. This formation had taken a beating during Halsey's September rampage. By October 20, not more than about 100 aircraft of all types were still operational.

Toyoda's plan called for the Second Air Fleet to reinforce the Philippines. This force was based in Kyushu, the Ryukyus, and Formosa under the command of Vice Admiral Fukudome. On October 10, it possessed the impressive total of 737 aircraft including 233 fighters. However, during the

IJN heavy cruisers carried a heavy main battery of between eight and ten 8in. guns. This is *Chokai* firing her main battery during exercises in 1933. Fire-control systems on board Japanese cruisers were good but depended on optical inputs since the Type 22 radar was not accurate enough for fire control.

This is an A6M5 "Zero" departing from a base in the Philippines for a suicide mission in October or November 1944. The A6M5 was the standard IJN fighter of the period, as well as the most numerous kamikaze aircraft. In the fighter role, the Zero was totally outclassed by the Hellcat. It was also limited in the special attack role since it could only carry the small 551lb bomb as seen in the photo. (Robert Lawson Collection, National Naval Aviation Museum)

period from October 10–20, the Second Air Fleet was heavily mauled by TF 38. From October 10–15, another 688 aircraft reinforced the Second Air Fleet. After the American invasion of Leyte, all possible reinforcements were moved from Formosa to the Philippines. All aircraft were planned to be in place for a massive strike against TF 38 on October 24. Accordingly, Fukudome flew to Manila on October 22 followed by 350 of his aircraft the next day. As will be seen, the IJN did succeed in mounting a large number or sorties on October 24. Following heavy losses from these attacks and readiness problems resulting from the fact that most of Fukudome's ground support personnel were still on Formosa, no additional large-scale attacks were possible.

Aircraft assigned to the two air fleets were dominated by the A6M5 "Zero" used in both fighter and fighter-bomber roles. The Zero was a prewar design. Though supremely maneuverable, it was thoroughly outclassed by the Hellcat by this point in the war. Strike aircraft were mainly D4Y "Judy" dive-bombers and a mix of longer-range bombers. These included the Mitsubishi G4M2 Type 1 Attack Bomber (Allied reporting name "Betty") that was still the IJN's standard long-range bomber despite its extreme vulnerability in daytime operations. Small numbers of the newer Yokosuka P1Y (Allied reporting name "Frances") bomber was also in service.

Another IJN mainstay aircraft during the Leyte campaign was the D4Y Carrier Bomber, given the Allied reporting name of "Judy." This is a D4Y3 conducting a suicide attack against carrier *Essex* on November 25, 1944. As the IJN's standard late-war dive-bomber, the Judy was used in conventional attacks, including the attack against *Princeton* on October 24, 1944 off Luzon. The Judy was fast (up to 357mph for the D4Y3) and could carry a decent payload. (NARA)

ORDERS OF BATTLE

UNITED STATES NAVY

THIRD FLEET

(Admiral William F. Halsey aboard *New Jersey*)

TASK FORCE 38

(Vice Admiral Marc A. Mitscher aboard *Lexington*)

The precise composition of the various task groups kept changing as ships, particularly destroyers, often changed subordination. Also, several ships had been detached after the Air Battle off Formosa to escort the torpedoed cruisers *Canberra* and *Houston* and were just returning to their original task groups. This is the best assessment of TF 38's composition on October 23, 1944.

Task Group 38.1 (Vice Admiral John S. McCain aboard *Wasp*)

Carriers:

Hancock	Air Group 7	
VB-7 (Bombing Squadron)	42 x SB2C-3/3E	
VF-7 (Fighter Squadron)	37 x F6F-5, 4 x F6F-5N	
VT-7 (Torpedo Squadron)	18 x TBM-1C	
Hornet	Air Group 11	
VB-11	25 x SB2C-3	
VF-11	40 x F6F-3/3N/3P/5/5N/5P	
VT-11	18 x TBM/TBF-1C	
Wasp	Air Group 14	1 x F6F-3
VB-14	10 x F6F-3/5, 25 x SB2C-3	
VF-14	42 x F6F-3/3N/3P/5/5N	
VT-14	18 x TBM/TBF-1C/1D	

Light carriers:

Monterey	Air Group 28	
VF-28	23 x F6F-5/5P	
VT-28	9 x TBM-1C	
Cowpens	Air Group 22	
VF-22	26 x F6F-5/5P	
VT-22	9 x TBM-1C	

Screen:

Heavy cruisers *Chester, Pensacola, Salt Lake City*

Destroyers *Bell, Boyd, Brown, Burns, Caperton, Case, Cassin, Charrette, Cogswell, Conner, Cowell, Cummings, Downes, Dunlap, Fanning, Grayson, Ingersoll, Izard, Knapp, McCalla, Woodworth*

Task Group 38.2 (Rear Admiral Gerald F. Bogan aboard *Intrepid*)

Carrier:

Intrepid	Air Group 18	1 x F6F-5
VB-18	28 x SB2C-3	
VF-18	43 x F6F-3N/5/5P	
VT-18	18 x TBM-1C	

Light carriers:

Cabot	Air Group 29
VF-29	21 x F6F-3/5
VT-29	9 x TBF/TBM-1C
Independence	Night Air Group 41
VFN-41	19 x F6F-3/5/5N
VTN-41	8 x TBM-1D

Screen:

Battleships *Iowa, New Jersey*

Light cruisers *Biloxi, Miami, Vincennes*

Destroyers *Benham, Colahan, Cushing, Halsey Powell, Hickox, Hunt, Lewis Hancock, Marshall, Miller, Owen, Stephen Potter, Stockham, The Sullivans, Tingey, Twining, Uhlmann, Wedderburn, Yarnell*

Task Group 38.3 (Rear Admiral Frederick C. Sherman aboard *Essex*)

Carriers:

Essex	Air Group 15	1 x F6F-3
VB-15	25 x SB2C-3	
VF-15	50 x F6F-3/3N/3P/5/5N	
VT-15	20 x TBF/TBM-1C	
Lexington	Air Group 19	1 x F6F-3
VB-19	30 x SB2C-3	
VF-19	41 x F6F-3/3N/3P/5/5N/5P	
VT-19	18 x TBM-1C	

Light carriers:

Langley	Air Group 44
VF-44	25 x F6F-3/5
VT-44	9 x TBM-1C
Princeton	Air Group 27
VF-27	25 x F6F-3/5
VT-27	9 x TBM-1C

Screen:

Battleships *Massachusetts, South Dakota*

Light cruisers *Birmingham, Mobile, Reno, Santa Fe*

Destroyers *Callaghan, Cassin Young, Clarence K. Bronson, Cotton, Dortch, Gatling, Healy, Porterfield, Preston*

Task Group 38.4 (Rear Admiral Ralph E. Davison aboard *Franklin*)

Carriers:

Enterprise	Air Group 20	1 x F6F-5
VB-20	34 x SB2C-3	
VF-20	39 x F6F-3N/5	
VT-20	19 x TBM-1C	
Franklin	Air Group 13	1 x F6F-5
VB-13	31 x SB2C-3	
VF-13	38 x F6F-3/3N/5/5N/5P	
VT-13	18 x TBM/TBF-1C	

Light carriers:

Belleau Wood	Air Group 21
VF-21	25 x F6F-3/5
VT-21	7 x TBM-1C
San Jacinto	Air Group 51
VF-51	25 x F6F-5/5P
VT-51	9 x TBM-1C

Screen:

Battleships *Alabama, Washington*

Heavy cruisers *New Orleans, Wichita*

Destroyers *Bagley, Gridley, Helm, Irwin, Laws, Longshaw, Maury, McCall, Morrison, Mugford, Nicholson, Patterson, Prichett, Ralph Talbot, Swanson, Wilkes*

SEVENTH FLEET

(Vice Admiral Thomas C. Kinkaid)

TASK GROUP 77.4 ESCORT CARRIER GROUP (REAR ADMIRAL THOMAS L. SPRAGUE)

Task Unit 77.4.1 "Taffy 1" (Rear Admiral Thomas L. Sprague)

Escort carriers:

Sangamon	Air Group 37	17 x F6F-3/5, 9 x TBM-1C
Suwannee	Air Group 60	22 x F6F-3, 9 x TBM-1C
Chenango	Air Group 35	22 x F6F-3, 9 x TBM-1C
Santee	Air Group 26	24 x FM-2, 9 x TBF/TBM-1C
Saginaw Bay	Composite Squadron 78	15 x FM-2, 12 x TBM-1C
Petrof Bay	Composite Squadron 76	16 x FM-2, 10 x TBM-1C

Screen:

Destroyers *McCord, Hazelwood, Trathen*

Destroyer escorts *Coolbaugh, Edmonds, Eversole, Richard M. Rowell, Richard S. Bull*

(Escort carriers *Chenango* and *Saginaw Bay* and destroyer escorts *Edmonds* and *Oberrender* detached at 1645hrs October 24, 1944.)

TU 77.4.2 "Taffy 2" (Rear Admiral Felix B. Stump)

Escort carriers:

Natoma Bay	Composite Squadron 81	16 x FM-2, 12 x TBM-1C
Manila Bay	Composite Squadron 80	16 x FM-2, 12 x TBM-1C
Marcus Island	Composite Squadron 21	12 x FM-2, 11 x TBM-1C
Kadashan Bay	Composite Squadron 20	15 x FM-2, 11 x TBM-1C
Savo Island	Composite Squadron 27	16 x FM-2, 12 x TBM-1C
Ommaney Bay	Composite Squadron 75	16 x FM-2, 11 x TBM-1C

Screen:
Destroyers *Franks, Haggard, Hailey*
Destroyer escorts *Abercrombie, Leray Wilson, Oberrender, Richard W. Suesens, Walter C. Wann*
TU 77.4.3 "Taffy 3" (Rear Admiral Clifton A. Sprague)
Escort carriers:

Fanshaw Bay	Composite Squadron 68	16 x FM-2, 12 x TBM-1C
St. Lo	Composite Squadron 65	17 x FM-2, 12 x TBM-1C
White Plains	Composite Squadron 4	16 x FM-2, 12 x TBM-1C
Kalinin Bay	Composite Squadron 3	16 x FM-2, 12 x TBF/TBM-1C
Kitkun Bay	Composite Squadron 5	14 x FM-2, 12 x TBM-1C
Gambier Bay	Composite Squadron 10	18 x FM-2, 12 x TBM-1C

Screen:
Destroyers *Hoel, Heermann, Johnston*
Destroyer escorts *Dennis, John C. Butler, Raymond, Samuel B. Roberts*
SUPPORTING SUBMARINES
Pacific Fleet—Task Force 17 (Vice Admiral Charles A. Lockwood)
Pintado, Jallao, Atule, Haddock, Halibut, Tuna, Sawfish, Drum, Icefish, Shark, Blackfish, Seadragon, Silversides, Salmon, Trigger, Besugo, Ronquil, Gabilan, Tang, Sterlet, Barbel, Snook
Seventh Fleet—Task Group 71.1 (Rear Admiral Ralph W. Christie)
Darter, Dace, Angler, Bluegill, Bream, Raton, Guitarro

IMPERIAL JAPANESE NAVY

FIRST DIVERSION ATTACK FORCE

(Vice Admiral Takeo Kurita aboard *Atago*)
First Section (Kurita)
1st *Sentai*[1]
    Battleships *Musashi, Nagato, Yamato*
4th *Sentai*
    Heavy cruisers *Atago, Chokai, Maya, Takao*
5th *Sentai*

1   *Sentai* was the IJN term for division.

    Heavy cruisers *Haguro, Myoko*
2nd Torpedo Flotilla
    Light cruiser *Noshiro*
    Destroyer *Shimakaze*
    2nd Torpedo Division
        Destroyers *Akishimo, Hayashimo*
    31st Torpedo Division
        Destroyers *Asashimo, Kishinami, Naganami, Okinami*
    32nd Torpedo Division
        Destroyers *Fujinami, Hamanami*
Second Section (Vice Admiral Yoshio Suzuki aboard *Kongo*)
3rd *Sentai*
    Battleships *Haruna, Kongo*
7th *Sentai*
    Heavy cruisers *Chikuma, Kumano, Suzuya, Tone*
10th Torpedo Flotilla
    Light cruiser *Yahagi*
    Destroyers *Kiyoshimo, Nowaki*
    17th Torpedo Division
        Destroyers *Hamakaze, Isokaze, Urakaze, Yukikaze*

LAND-BASED AIR FORCES[2]

5th Base Air Force (1st Air Fleet) (Vice Admiral Takijiro Onishi)
(Number of operational aircraft fluctuated; on October 24, 1944 about 60 were operational.)
6th Base Air Force (2nd Air Fleet) (Vice Admiral Shigeru Fukudome)
    202nd Air Group (fighters)
    341st Air Group (fighters)
    763rd Air Group (medium bombers)
    141st Air Group (dive-bombers, reconnaissance aircraft, night-fighters)
(Approximately 350 aircraft had arrived in the Philippines by October 23, 1944; approximately 200 were operational.)

2   On October 25, 1944 the 5th and 6th Base Air Forces were unified under the 1st Combined Base Air Force.

Kongo was the lead ship in a class of battlecruisers built during World War I and converted into fast battleships between the wars. This is a photograph of *Kongo* running sea trials in November 1936 following modernization. Her speed allowed her to aggressively pursue Taffy 3 off Samar on October 25, 1944.

OPPOSING PLANS

THE AMERICAN PLAN

There was little attempt to deceive the Japanese in the lead-up to the Leyte invasion. Marcus Island was shelled on October 9 in the hopes that it might convince the Japanese that the Bonin Islands were the next target. The British conducted a raid on the Nicobar Islands in the Indian Ocean between October 17 and 21 to make the Japanese consider a threat to their western flank. Both diversions failed to make an impression on the Japanese.

The landing on Leyte was scheduled for October 20 with an invasion force consisting of two corps. Each had its own landing area on the eastern coast of Leyte and each beachhead was covered by strong naval forces.

From a naval standpoint, the command structure for the invasion was convoluted. The Seventh Fleet, part of MacArthur's Southwest Area Command, supplied the forces for the invasion, including the Northern and Southern Attack forces slated to deliver the two corps on Leyte. Significant naval forces were embedded in these two forces to provide naval gunfire support, air defense for the beachhead, and to defeat any local Japanese naval incursions. Part of the covering force was a group of 18 escort carriers.

The bulk of American naval power resided in the Third Fleet, which was still under Nimitz's command. The mission of the Third Fleet was to provide cover and support for the landings. This would be done in several phases. From October 10 to 13, the carriers would strike Okinawa, Formosa, and northern Luzon to reduce Japanese air power. From October 16 to 20, as the landing neared, the carriers would shift their attention to Leyte and the central Philippines. After the landings, TF 38 would operate in "strategic support" by destroying Japanese air and naval forces that threatened the invasion.

This schedule was created by agreement with MacArthur's staff. It was always clear that TF 38 was not under MacArthur's command. The divided chain of command for the naval forces was bad enough, but a real potential for miscommunication between Halsey and Kinkaid was created in the details

John C. Butler pictured on May 29, 1944 off Boston Navy Yard where she was built shortly after being commissioned. This fine view shows her main armament consisting of two 5in./38 single mounts and a triple mount of torpedo tubes. *John C. Butler* was the lead ship in a class of 83 units.

Principal IJN Forces involved in the *Sho-1* plan

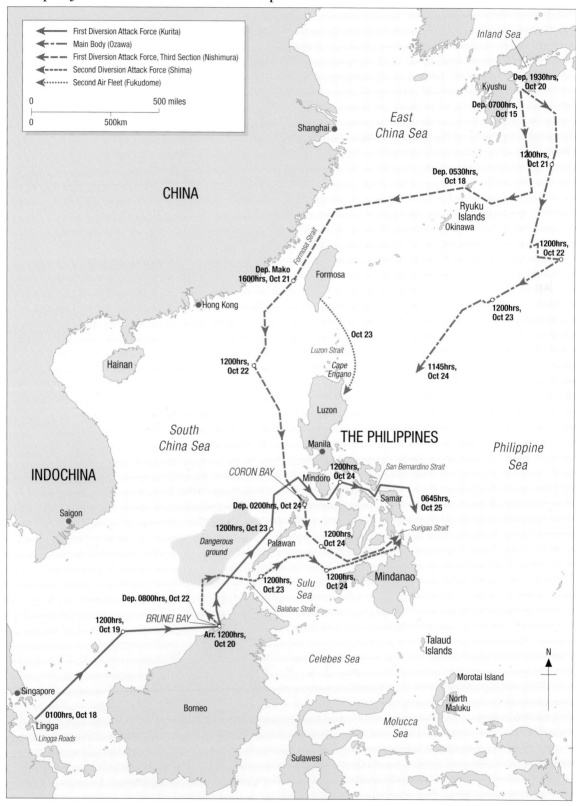

Legend:
- First Diversion Attack Force (Kurita)
- Main Body (Ozawa)
- First Diversion Attack Force, Third Section (Nishimura)
- Second Diversion Attack Force (Shima)
- Second Air Fleet (Fukudome)

0 — 500 miles
0 — 500km

Inland Sea

Dep. 1930hrs, Oct 20
Kyushu
Dep. 0700hrs, Oct 15

Dep. 0530hrs, Oct 18

East China Sea

Shanghai ●

1200hrs, Oct 21

CHINA

Ryuku Islands
Okinawa

1200hrs, Oct 22

Formosa Strait

Dep. Mako 1600hrs, Oct 21
Formosa

● Hong Kong

1200hrs, Oct 23

1145hrs, Oct 24

Hainan

Luzon Strait
Oct 23
Cape Engano

1200hrs, Oct 22

Luzon

THE PHILIPPINES

Philippine Sea

Manila ●

South China Sea

INDOCHINA

San Bernardino Strait

CORON BAY
Mindoro
1200hrs, Oct 24
Samar
0645hrs, Oct 25

Dep. 0200hrs, Oct 24

Saigon ●

1200hrs, Oct 23
Dangerous ground
Palawan
1200hrs, Oct 24

Surigao Strait

1200hrs, Oct 23
Sulu Sea
1200hrs, Oct 24
Mindanao

Balabac Strait

Dep. 0800hrs, Oct 22
BRUNEI BAY

Talaud Islands

N

1200hrs, Oct 19
Arr. 1200hrs, Oct 20

Morotai Island

● Singapore

Celebes Sea

North Maluku

0100hrs, Oct 18
Lingga
Lingga Roads

Borneo

Molucca Sea

Sulawesi ●

of Halsey's orders. In Nimitz's operation plan, he directed Halsey to make destruction of the Japanese fleet his primary task if the situation offered itself. This instruction was incorporated by Halsey into his operational plan. It was the direct outgrowth of the just-concluded Battle of the Philippine Sea during which Admiral Spruance decided not to take the fast carrier force to pre-empt a Japanese attack, but instead allowed the Japanese to mount a series of air attacks and then escape destruction. It goes without saying that the Third Fleet had the responsibility to protect the landing from a Japanese attack, but Nimitz made it clear that if the Japanese fleet made another appearance, then its destruction was Halsey's primary mission. There is no doubt that Halsey would have attacked the Japanese fleet even in the absence of direct orders to do so, but with his explicit orders to do so there was the potential he would act in such a way to leave the beachhead vulnerable to Japanese attack.

THE JAPANESE PLAN

While the Americans debated whether and when to land in the Philippines, the Japanese had few doubts that the Philippines would be next. As early as March 1944, the Imperial General Headquarters had seen the American advances through the Central Pacific and up from the Southwest Pacific converging on the Philippines. This was all but confirmed by the June landing on Saipan and the April invasion of Hollandia on New Guinea. The Japanese did not know which Philippines island would be the target of the American landing, but they were sure the Philippines were next and that the landing would occur in mid-November (the schedule of the original American plan).

Defense of the Philippines was critical to Japan's ability to continue the war. The loss of the Marianas forced the Japanese back to their inner defense line of the Home Islands, the Ryukyus, Formosa, the Philippines, and the Netherlands East Indies. If this line could be held, Japanese war industry could continue to produce essential war materials. If the inner defense line was penetrated, then oil and other resources could not be moved to the Home Islands and the war would be lost. The Japanese assessed that the highest priority in their inner defense line was holding the Philippines. The Japanese envisioned an attack on the Philippines as early as mid-November. The exact target remained unclear until mid-October, when they decided that an attack on Leyte was most likely.

Accordingly, the Philippines were given top priority for preparations for an anticipated "general decisive battle." The plan for the decisive battle was designated *Sho-Go* (*Victory Operation*). American invasions of the Philippines, Formosa–Ryukyus, Honshu–Kyushu, and Hokkaido–Kuriles were given separate variants of the *Sho* plan. *Sho-1* was the plan for the Philippines and was the one seen by the Japanese as most likely.

Though the Japanese had discerned the target of the American invasion and its approximate date, they lacked any information on the invasion's precise timing. This was crucial since it meant that *Sho-1* could not be activated until American intentions were clear. Here was the Achilles heel of *Sho-1*. Because the exact timing of the American invasion was unknown, and given the distance that any Japanese attack force had to travel from its base near Singapore, the earliest the IJN could attack the landing force was a week after the activation of *Sho-1*. This in turn meant that the invasion force

A major part of any IJN decisive battle plan was its force of destroyers. These ships were powerful torpedo platforms carrying eight Type 93 torpedoes and eight reloads. This is *Naganami*, a Yugumo-class unit. (Shizuo Fukui, Kure Maritime Museum)

would be undisturbed for that period allowing it to unload the invasion force and necessary supplies before safely withdrawing. *Sho-1* could never destroy the invasion force or stop the landing.

Admiral Toyoda had a weak hand to play for *Sho-1*. After the debacle at the Battle of the Philippine Sea, the IJN's heavy units returned to Lingga Roads to train for the next decisive battle but, more importantly, to be near their source of oil. The defeated carrier force was sent to the Inland Sea where it could train new air groups without fear of submarine attack. Had the invasion of the Philippines been delayed until November, the new carrier groups would have been declared ready and the carriers would also have deployed to Lingga to join the surface forces. With no carriers ready and a weak land-based air force, Toyoda needed a new plan. What he and his staff devised was clever but fell far short of being able to defeat the American invasion. In early October, the Japanese revised their intelligence assessment to include an American landing in the Philippines during the last ten days of the month with Leyte as the probable landing place.

Toyoda's plan centered on the First Diversion Attack Force and its ability to get into Leyte Gulf to attack the American invasion force. Commanded by Vice Admiral Kurita, this force included seven battleships (including *Yamato* and *Musashi*), 11 heavy cruisers, two light cruisers, and 19 destroyers. This impressive collection of firepower was divided into three sections. The first two, with five battleships, ten heavy cruisers, two light cruisers, and 15 destroyers, under Kurita's direct command, would transit the Sibuyan Sea, pass through the San Bernardino Strait into the Philippine Sea, and then enter Leyte Gulf from the north. The third section, with the two slowest battleships, a heavy cruiser, and four destroyers, under Vice Admiral Nishimura, would transit Surigao Strait and enter Leyte Gulf from the south coincident with the movement of Kurita's force. Another smaller force, acting independently under Vice Admiral Shima, was designated the Second Diversion Attack Force and was also ordered to enter Leyte Gulf through Surigao Strait. Incredibly, Shima and Nishimura did not coordinate their operations, even though their forces would be passing through the same narrow body of water toward the same objective.

Any movement by Kurita into Leyte Gulf was at the mercy of Halsey's Third Fleet. The success of *Sho-1* depended on the Japanese finding a way to neutralize the Third Fleet. The preferred method was the use of land-based air power, but the perilous state of Japanese air power in the Philippines offered little chance of success. Onishi and Fukudome decided to use all their strength for offensive operations against the Third Fleet leaving nothing for air cover of Kurita's force. Realizing that his land-based air forces were

First Diversion Attack Force, October 20–28, 1944

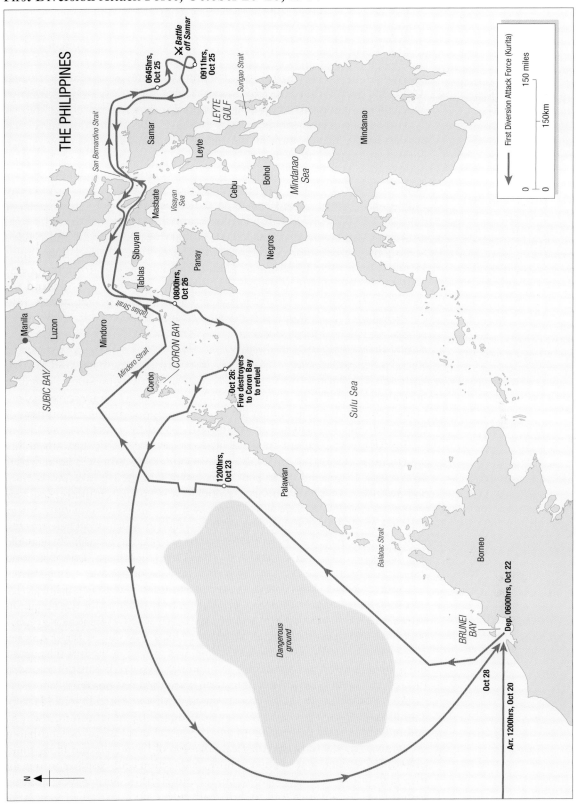

THE PHILIPPINES

X *Battle off Samar*

0645hrs, Oct 25

0911hrs, Oct 25

Surigao Strait

Samar

LEYTE GULF

Leyte

Mindanao

San Bernardino Strait

Masbate

Cebu

Bohol

Mindanao Sea

Visayan Sea

Sibuyan

Tablas

Negros

Panay

Tablas Strait

0800hrs, Oct 26

Luzon

Mindoro

Mindoro Strait

CORON BAY

Coron

Oct 26: Five destroyers to Coron Bay to refuel

Manila

SUBIC BAY

Sulu Sea

1200hrs, Oct 23

Palawan

Dangerous ground

Balabac Strait

Borneo

Dep. 0600hrs, Oct 22

BRUNEI BAY

Oct 28

Arr. 1200hrs, Oct 20

First Diversion Attack Force (Kurita)

150 miles

150km

N

too weak to neutralize Halsey's forces, Toyoda's primary plan for dealing with Halsey was using the Mobile Force's Main Body, under Vice Admiral Ozawa, to lure Halsey's carriers to the north opening the door for Kurita to storm into Leyte Gulf. The Main Body was comprised of the remnants of the IJN's carrier force—one fleet carrier, three light carriers, and two battleships converted into hybrid carriers by removing their after main gun turrets and replacing them with a short flight deck. This force was only capable of diversionary operations since it carried only 116 aircraft.

Timing was critical for the success of *Sho-1*. The Main Body's diversion mission had to be accomplished in time to save the First Diversion Attack Force from getting pounded by American carrier aircraft as it transited the Sibuyan Sea. The Main Body departed its bases in the Inland Sea on October 20 and exited the Bungo Strait that evening undetected by American submarines. Kurita's force had departed earlier, leaving Lingga Roads at 0100hrs on October 18. It headed for Brunei Bay for refueling and a final pre-attack conference. Then it left at 0800hrs on October 22 and headed toward the Philippines. Nishimura's section departed Brunei that day at 1500hrs. If all went according to plan, both forces would storm into Leyte Gulf on the morning of October 25. Presaging the final approach of the Japanese forces, the land-based forces in the Philippines would make an all-out attack on the American carriers on October 24.

Assessment of Operation Sho-1

Sho-1 had no prospects of success. The disparity in strength between the two fleets was too marked to allow the IJN to accomplish its mission of repelling the American invasion. The clever diversionary aspect to the plan and its success should not camouflage the basic weakness of *Sho-1*. Any prospect for success was undermined by the uncertainty of the exact time and place of the American landing. As a result, Kurita's force could not attack the landings in its most vulnerable phase but would only arrive days later, even if everything went according to plan. This meant that the IJN was committing its remaining strength against heavy odds just for the opportunity to attack empty transports and follow-up supply and reinforcement echelons, not to crush the landing force before it got ashore. Another salient weakness was the underlying premise that surface forces could operate without air cover while moving significant distances under air attack and still achieve their objectives. Still another serious flaw was the high level of coordination among forces spread over a wide area. The intricate nature of the plan was typical of IJN operational planning, and just as it had during every other major IJN operation of the war, the forces at Leyte would experience severe communication and coordination issues that placed the entire plan at risk. In the final analysis, *Sho-1* contained only the seeds for the final destruction of the IJN. The Third Fleet could not be neutralized, only temporarily diverted. If Kurita's force did succeed in reaching Leyte Gulf, and after it attacked low-value transports, it would be caught in the gulf between the Seventh and Third fleets and likely annihilated. Thus, *Sho-1* had no chance of reversing the course of the war and risked the utter destruction of the IJN in the process. Toyoda probably should have waited until the American invasion of Luzon, giving the Japanese a chance to regenerate their carrier force and position land-based air power on the island's many airfields. Instead, he committed the IJN's remaining strength to a rash plan that turned out to be a death ride.

THE BATTLE

THE AIR BATTLE OFF FORMOSA

The true beginning of the Battle for Leyte occurred a week before the First Diversion Attack Force departed on its fateful sortie. When the Third Fleet conducted a series of pre-invasion strikes to reduce Japanese land-based air power, the Japanese activated the land-based air forces allocated to *Sho-1* and *Sho-2* to deal with Halsey's incursion. TF 38 rendezvoused west of the Marianas on October 7 and headed west for scheduled strikes on October 10 against Okinawa and the Ryukyus. Almost 1,400 sorties pounded targets on Okinawa and the Ryukyus throughout the day on October 10. In response, Toyoda ordered a major effort to attack Halsey's fleet. Considerable forces were allocated to this effort. In total, 1,425 aircraft were committed, including those from Formosa, Okinawa, and Luzon, but also pulled from China (31), northern Japan (250), the carrier air groups of the Mobile Fleet (172), and 200 Imperial Army aircraft on Formosa. Among these was the "T" (Typhoon) Attack Force of Imperial Navy and Army bombers trained for maritime attack missions. The Japanese hoped this seemingly impressive display of air power would cripple the Third Fleet, or at least force a delay in the invasion of the Philippines.

After a diversion to strike Aparri Airfield on northern Luzon on October 11, TF 38 moved to a position only 50–90NM east of Formosa to launch a series of attacks on October 12. Four strikes were conducted during the day preceded by a fighter sweep. The Hellcats quickly gained air control over Formosa against the 230 Japanese fighters on the island. By the third strike of the day, the Americans faced no air opposition. The almost 1,400 sorties on October 12 were followed by almost 1,000 more the next day, and 246 on October 14. In addition to defeating the defending fighters, Japanese airfields and other facilities were heavily damaged.

The real story of the battle off Formosa was the series of Japanese air attacks on TF 38. The T Force attempted to strike back with dusk and night attacks on October 12. According to Japanese sources, 101 sorties were flown with 42 aircraft lost. Reports from the attacking aviators were optimistic though, indicating that four carriers were sunk (this was reduced the next day to two carriers). On October 13, the air groups of Carrier Division 3 and 4 arrived on Formosa to increase the weight of attacks. At twilight, the T Force mounted additional strikes against TG 38.1 and TG 38.4 with 43 aircraft; 20 were lost. *Franklin* was attacked by a small group of G4M medium bombers at dusk that were able to close on the carrier undetected by radar. Though their torpedoes missed, one Betty crashed on the carrier's deck, causing minor damage. Using the tactic of attacking from low level at twilight, a group of B6N2 "Jill" torpedo bombers struck while the American carriers were recovering aircraft. The Jills flew low enough to escape detection on radar. Eight came in, six were dealt with by antiaircraft fire, but one lined up for a torpedo launch on heavy cruiser *Canberra*. The torpedo struck the cruiser in a vulnerable spot—under the main armor belt between both firerooms. The ship lost all power, laying just 90NM off Formosa. Halsey decided to take the cruiser in tow and detached two light carriers, five cruisers, and 12 destroyers to cover her withdrawal. A major strike of 170 Imperial Navy and Army aircraft from the Philippines miscarried when it failed to find a target.

The Japanese mounted their biggest effort on October 14 with over 400 sorties in several waves. A total of 360 daylight sorties were flown from Formosa. The first wave failed to find a target, and the third wave was called off and failed to attack. The second wave ran into the CAP of TG 38.2 and TG 38.3 and was mauled. The only bright spot for the Japanese was another twilight attack by the T Force by 52 aircraft against TG 38.1. Four Jills broke through to attack light cruiser *Houston*. Three were shot down, but the last succeeded in placing a torpedo in another vulnerable spot that flooded the engineering spaces and caused all power to be lost. The ship was almost abandoned but was eventually taken in tow.

Exaggerated reports of success from Japanese aviators led Toyoda to order further attacks. Almost 200 sorties were flown on October 15 from bases on Luzon, Formosa, and Okinawa. The strike from Luzon consisted of some 90 aircraft targeted against TG 38.4. The strike was intercepted by Hellcats and only minor damage was inflicted on *Franklin*. On the afternoon of October 16, the Japanese directed their attacks on the two crippled cruisers and their escorts. Hellcats from light carriers *Cabot* and *Cowpens* did great execution against a Japanese formation of over 100 aircraft. However, three Jills penetrated the screen and put another torpedo into *Houston*. The ship had some 6,300 tons of water on board, but the cruiser's crew refused to let her sink. These were the last Japanese attacks before the two crippled cruisers pulled out of air range.

A Japanese B6N "Jill" torpedo bomber plane passes the starboard quarter of *Essex* after dropping its torpedo on October 14, 1944. In the background is a South Dakota-class battleship. The inability of the Japanese to mass aircraft against TF 38 and the inexperience of almost all of the Japanese aviators during the Air Battle off Formosa meant the Japanese took very heavy losses for little return in the run-up to the Battle of Leyte Gulf.

The series of air attacks was the heaviest of the war to date by the Japanese against the USN. A total of 761 offensive sorties were flown with 321 aircraft lost, according to Japanese sources. In total, the Japanese admitted to the loss of 492 aircraft, but TF 38 claims totaled 655. In exchange for their heavy losses, the Japanese claimed a great victory with 11 American carriers sunk and many other ships sunk or damaged. In reality, only the two cruisers were damaged. In addition, the USN lost 76 aircraft in combat and 13 due to operational causes.

Light cruiser *Houston* photographed under tow on October 17, 1944 after being torpedoed twice by Japanese aircraft during operations off Formosa. Heavy cruiser *Canberra* was also torpedoed off Formosa and can be seen under tow in the distance. These were the only TF 38 ships damaged in the battle, despite Japanese claims that the Third Fleet had suffered crippling losses.

Japanese land-based air forces had mounted an all-out effort between October 12 and 16 to crush the Third Fleet and had totally failed. The attacks were conducted in a fragmented manner against the numerically superior TF 38. Radar-directed Hellcats easily defeated the piecemeal attacks. No delay was forced on the American timetable and no significant damage inflicted on TF 38. This failure had direct implications for Japanese hopes of successfully defending the Philippines. The impotence of and attrition inflicted on the IJN's land-based air forces reduced the chances of success for *Sho-1* to zero. Now the First Diversion Attack Force would operate without air cover and the Mobile Force was reduced to a mere decoy.

SHO-1 IS ACTIVATED

Because of the distances involved and the uncertain fuel situation for the main fleet at Lingga Roads, Toyoda had to be sure the Americans were landing before he activated *Sho-1* and committed the surface fleet. Kurita was given a warning order to prepare for operations on October 16. The Japanese assessment that Leyte was the American target was confirmed the next morning when observers on Suluan Island in the eastern approaches to Leyte Gulf reported the approach of American naval forces. Armed with this knowledge, Toyoda ordered all forces allocated for *Sho-1* to go on alert. The First Diversion Attack Force was ordered to proceed to Brunei. Just after midnight on October 18, Kurita's ships departed Lingga anchorage and began their trek to Leyte. *Sentai* (Division) 16—heavy cruiser *Aoba*, light cruiser *Kinu*, and destroyer *Uranami*—was ordered to detach from Kurita's command and head to Manila. These ships were all among the oldest in Kurita's fleet, but it was a mistake to detach them for a secondary transport mission when they would have been better used to augment the decisive attack planned for Kurita's force.

Once he was absolutely sure of the American intent to invade Leyte, Toyoda issued orders to execute *Sho-1* at 1110hrs on October 18. The attack into Leyte Gulf to crush the American landing force was set for the morning of October 25. This would be too late to catch the invasion force or to hit the invasion fleet in the vulnerable process of landing troops. The American landings at two points on Leyte occurred on schedule on the morning of October 20. Opposition on the ground was weak with only some 50 American casualties recorded on the northern beaches. However,

Kurita's First Diversion Attack Force leaves Brunei Bay just after 0800hrs on October 22, 1944. The ships in this photograph are from the First Section and include, right to left, battleships *Nagato*, *Musashi*, and *Yamato*; and heavy cruisers *Maya*, *Chokai*, *Takao*, *Atago*, *Haguro*, and *Myoko*. Only three of these ships returned to Brunei at the end of the operation on October 28.

a Japanese aircraft surprised light cruiser *Honolulu*; the ship took a torpedo hit and suffered 60 men killed. Flooding caused a temporary severe list, but the ship was saved by efficient damage measures. But *Honolulu* was out of the fight.

The assault ships were quickly unloaded and departed by evening on October 20. The first reinforcement echelon arrived on October 22 and finished unloading that same afternoon. Reinforcement Group 2 arrived on October 24. This was a large force of 33 LSTs, 24 Liberty ships, and ten support ships escorted by four destroyers and two frigates. Of these, most were still present on October 25 and were ordered to wait inside the gulf until the battles that day were concluded. At midnight on October 24, shipping inside Leyte Gulf totaled three flagships, one assault transport, 23 LSTs, two medium landing ships, and 28 Liberty ships.

However, the invasion force was safely ashore with a total of 132,400 men and just under 200,000 tons of supplies. This fact meant the *Sho-1* plan was pointless since the invasion force was already firmly ashore with enough supplies for sustained operations.

As the landings proceeded about as smoothly as could be hoped, Halsey held the bulk of TF 38 northeast of Luzon through October 19 in the aftermath of the Formosa air battle to provide escort for the two crippled cruisers. TGs 38.1 and 38.4 fueled on October 21 and then were ordered to head to Ulithi the following day. As it became apparent the IJN was mounting a major operation, Halsey ordered TG 38.4 to turn back toward Leyte on October 23, but TG 38.1 continued until being recalled on the 24th.

The First Diversion Attack Force departed Lingga at 0100hrs on October 18 and headed to Brunei Bay on the north coast of Borneo. At Brunei, Kurita's ships refueled, and Kurita took the opportunity to confer with his officers. The details of *Sho-1* reached Kurita's force during the day on October 18. This made for a dramatic conference and reflected the unease many felt about the plan. Many officers at the conference were appalled that the fleet was being risked attacking empty transports and doubted that they would ever get close to Leyte Gulf. Kurita probably had his own doubts about the plan, but after many of those present expressed their doubts, Kurita reminded them of the "glorious opportunity" they had been given. "Would it not be a shame to have the fleet remain intact while the nation perishes?" posed Kurita, and followed with the plea: "What man can say that there is no chance for our fleet to turn the tide of war in a decisive battle?"

Whatever their doubts, the crews and ships of the First Diversion Attack Force departed Brunei at 0800hrs on October 22 and headed northeast through the Palawan Passage. Kurita's Third Section—consisting of the old battleships *Fuso* and *Yamashiro*, heavy cruiser *Mogami*, and four destroyers—stayed behind. These ships departed at 1500hrs and headed to the Balabac Strait and then into the Sulu Sea. If all went according to plan, they would storm Leyte Gulf through the Surigao Strait and meet Kurita's ships inside the gulf on the morning of October 25.

AMBUSH AT PALAWAN

Kurita had three potential routes from Brunei to San Bernardino Strait. The shortest route was through the Sulu Sea, but this was within range of American long-range search aircraft from Morotai, so was rejected. The other two routes went through the Mindoro Strait. The most direct route was along the west coast of Palawan. The final route was farther to the west over an area known as the Dangerous Ground. Because the last route required another refueling and would put him behind the schedule set by the Combined Fleet, Kurita chose the direct route to the Mindoro Strait. This was an area where American submarines were known to operate.

For its transit to San Bernardino Strait, the First Diversion Attack Force was divided into two sections. The lead section consisted of the three most powerful battleships, the heavy cruisers of *Sentai* 4 and 5, escorted by the destroyers of Torpedo Flotilla 2. The second section was some 4NM behind with the two Kongo-class battleships, the heavy cruisers of *Sentai* 7, and the destroyers of Torpedo Flotilla 10. During the afternoon of October 22, there were three reports of submarines, all false alarms. That night, Kurita reduced his speed to 16 knots and ceased zigzagging. At daybreak, speed was increased to 18 knots and the formation resumed zigzagging.

The Japanese had good reason to be concerned about enemy submarines. A shortage of destroyers made Kurita's force vulnerable to submarine attack, and he compounded the problem by failing to place a destroyer out in front of his formation to clear the way through waters known to be submarine infested. It was an obvious choice for the Americans to place submarines in the southern entrance of the Palawan Passage. In fact, there were two submarines positioned there, *Darter* and *Dace*. Both were under the tactical control of *Darter*'s skipper, Commander David H. McClintock. Commander Bladen D. Claggett commanded *Dace*. At 0116hrs on October 23, *Darter*'s radar picked up the approaching Japanese 15NM distant. As was the practice for USN submarines in 1944, they aggressively moved at over 20 knots to close the contact. The two submarines raced up the 30NM-wide Palawan Passage to get ahead of the Japanese. Soon, they gained visual contact and sent the first of three contact reports. These were passed to Halsey and Kinkaid with a final estimate that the large task force contained 11 heavy ships and six destroyers.

After *Darter*'s contact reports were picked up by the Japanese, Kurita ordered his ships to be on the lookout for submarines. Even at this point, he failed to send any destroyers to clear the route for his force. *Darter* and *Dace* moved into perfect attack positions—*Darter* to attack the port column of heavy ships led by *Atago* with Kurita aboard, while *Dace* laid in wait to strike the starboard column. Beginning at 0610hrs, the submarines dived to conduct a coordinated attack. At a range of just under 1,000 yards, McClintock fired his six bow tubes. After maneuvering his boat 180°, McClintock fired his four stern tubes just as the first of the bow torpedoes found their mark.

The first torpedoes struck *Atago* just as Kurita was having morning tea with his chief of staff. In total, four torpedoes hit the cruiser, dooming her instantly. Nineteen officers and 341 sailors went down with the ship. Kurita and his staff were thrown into the water and had to swim for their lives. The second salvo from *Darter* hit cruiser *Takao*, steaming behind *Atago*. Two

AMBUSH IN THE PALAWAN PASSAGE (PP. 42–43)

Kurita expected heavy American resistance as his force headed for Leyte Gulf. The first blow was struck on October 24 in the Palawan Passage where submarines *Darter* and *Dace* were positioned. After picking up the Japanese force on radar at 0116hrs, *Darter* made a contact report and raced up the Palawan Passage at full speed to get in front of the Japanese to mount an attack. No Japanese destroyers were encountered, and the Japanese failed to pick up the surfaced American submarine on radar.

Commander McClintock, *Darter*'s skipper, planned to attack at first light. At 0610hrs, *Darter* submerged and prepared to attack the left column of heavy ships in Kurita's First Section. This column was led by Kurita's flagship *Atago*. McClintock changed course to

parallel the column so he could fire his bow and stern torpedo tubes without having to turn completely around. At a range of just under 1,000 yards, McClintock fired his six bow tubes at *Atago*. He quickly maneuvered *Darter* 180° and brought his aft tubes to bear on the next cruiser in line. Just as heavy explosions were registered from the first salvo, the first of the stern torpedoes left their tubes.

In this illustration, *Atago* (**1**) is on fire having been hit by four torpedoes. At 0634hrs, just a minute after *Atago* was hit, *Takao* (**2**) was hit by two torpedoes. One struck in the area of the bridge, and the second on the stern. The burning *Atago* sank within 18 minutes of being hit. *Takao* survived and limped to Singapore, where she was deemed beyond repair.

torpedoes hit the cruiser, killing 32 crewmen and wounding another 30. *Takao* was not only out of the battle, but her heavy damage put her out of the war. After eventually reaching Singapore, she was deemed unrepairable.

On *Dace*, Claggett observed *Darter*'s devastating attack. Claggett identified a Kongo-class battleship for attack and began his approach. Six torpedoes were fired from a range of 1,800 yards toward the target, which was actually heavy cruiser *Maya*. The cruiser took four hits on her port side and sank in a mere eight minutes, taking with her 16 officers and 320 men. Both submarines survived ineffective counterattacks from Japanese destroyers. *Darter* attempted to finish off *Takao* but was unable to get close enough for another attack. As *Darter* stalked *Takao* that night, she ran hard aground on a reef. Despite McClintock's best efforts, the submarine could not be freed. The crew was transferred to *Dace*.

This brilliant attack by *Darter* and *Dace* not only reduced Kurita's force by three powerful cruisers, but it gave the Americans the location of the First Diversion Attack Force. Two destroyers were lost to Kurita when he dispatched them to escort the crippled *Takao* back to Brunei. Kurita's trial by fire was just beginning. He was picked up by destroyer *Kishinami* and eventually transferred to *Yamato* that afternoon. He said later that his swim "actually brought me a good result. I felt much better and I could lead the battles in a good mood." Kurita lost three-quarters of his communications staff, which had an impact for the rest of the battle.

Gato-class submarine *Darter* photographed aground on Bombay Shoal where she came to grief on the morning of October 24 while attempting to finish off the damaged heavy cruiser *Takao*. The wreck remained essentially intact in this position until 1962.

THE JAPANESE AIR ATTACKS

On October 23, most of the Second Air Fleet's aircraft flew to the Philippines from Formosa. This was a precursor to mass attacks the next day on TF 38 to provide indirect protection for the First Diversion Attack Force. No effort was made to provide Kurita's force with air cover. This was pointless given the level of training by the aviators and the persistent issues with communications.

It was crucial that the American carriers be neutralized since Kurita's and Ozawa's forces would come within range of TF 38 on October 24.

No search operations were possible on October 23 because of poor weather. On October 24, the weather east of Luzon was still heavy, but a search aircraft located American carriers at 0820hrs. This was TG 38.3 with its four carriers, which was the closest task group to the airfields on Luzon. All of the Japanese attacks on October 24 were directed against it. Over 200 sorties were made, but not all of these aircraft found a target because of the weather. Three attack waves were formed, each with some 50–60 aircraft.

On October 23, 1944, the Japanese made another all-out effort to cripple TF 38. The effort failed, but did result in the sinking of *Princeton*. This is the light carrier burning after one bomb hit resulted in heavy explosions on the carrier's hangar deck.

The first attack in the morning was intercepted by seven Hellcats from *Essex* led by Commander David McCampbell, the air group commander. The quality of the Japanese air crews was very low. McCampbell methodically proceeded to shoot down nine Japanese aircraft, for which he was awarded the Congressional Medal of Honor, and his wingman claimed six more. Altogether, aviators from *Essex* were credited with 24 downed enemy aircraft, and fighters from *Lexington* 13.

Despite the Hellcats' rough handling of the incoming Japanese strike, fleet air defense was never airtight. At 0938hrs, one Judy dive-bomber used clouds for cover and then made a skillful attack against light carrier *Princeton*. The aircraft's 551lb bomb hit in the middle of the flight deck some 75ft forward of the aft elevator. It penetrated several decks to the ship's bakery, where it exploded. The resulting blast reached into the hangar deck where it engulfed six fully armed and fully fueled Avengers. These aircraft caught fire and soon exploded with a blast so powerful both ship's elevators were thrown into the air. Water pressure was knocked out, which allowed the flames to spread quickly. All non-essential personnel were ordered off the ship at 1010hrs, followed by all but the fire-fighting personnel ten minutes later.

As explosions racked *Princeton*, other ships were ordered to stand by to assist her. Light cruiser *Birmingham* came alongside at 1100hrs and 38 of her crew went over to the carrier to fight fires. With progress being made, the decision was taken to tow the carrier to Ulithi. However, a persistent fire near the stern resisted efforts to extinguish it, and it gained strength when *Birmingham* was forced to cast off at 1212hrs when a Japanese submarine contact was reported. The cruiser came back at 1445hrs to resume fighting the fire. She was closing to rig a tow line when at 1523hrs the fires reached the torpedo magazine aft. A major explosion resulted that shattered *Princeton*'s stern and her after flight deck. Devastation was also wrought on the topsides of *Birmingham*—229 crewmen were killed and 420 wounded—more than half the cruiser's complement. *Birmingham* was forced to go to Ulithi for repairs, but *Princeton*'s fate was worse. No other ships in the task group were able to rig a tow line and the fires on the carrier raged unchecked. Sherman ordered her scuttled. After some difficulty, this was accomplished at 1746hrs. *Princeton* was the first fast carrier lost since October 1942, and the last to be sunk in the war.

Though *Princeton*'s demise was undeniably a Japanese success, the massive air strike planned by Fukudome and Onishi to neutralize TF 38 was an undeniable failure. Only TG 38.3 had been found and detected. This only delayed the launching of a strike by Sherman's task group against Kurita's force until about 1050hrs. Failure to inflict serious damage against TF 38 left Kurita's force totally exposed.

THE BATTLE OF THE SIBUYAN SEA

By October 23, three major IJN formations had been spotted heading toward Leyte, confirming that a major Japanese effort was underway. Despite his best efforts to make the Americans aware of his presence, Ozawa's carrier force had yet to be detected. Halsey initially doubted that the Japanese would mount a major operation in response to the American invasion. When the Japanese did just that, Halsey did not have TF 38 in the best position to respond. Halsey ordered TG 38.2, TG 38.3, and TG 38.4 to be ready to launch search aircraft and strikes on October 24. Of these, only TG 38.2 would be in an immediate position to strike Kurita's force. TG 38.1 was still on its way to Ulithi to replenish until being recalled on the morning of October 24.

Reformed after the debacle in the Palawan Passage, the First Diversion Attack Force entered the Mindoro Strait. An American submarine spotted Kurita's force after midnight on October 24 but could not make an attack. Just after 0800hrs, search aircraft from TG 38.2 reported Kurita's force south of Mindoro. Halsey waited only five minutes after receiving the contact report to issue orders to the Third Fleet for operations on October 24. Because TG 38.3 was too far north and TG 38.4 was too far south to immediately strike, TG 38.2 carried the initial burden for striking Kurita's force. This was not an ideal situation since TG 38.2 was the weakest of Halsey's four task groups with only fleet carrier *Intrepid* and light carriers *Cabot* and *Independence*. TG 38.2's actual striking power was further reduced since *Independence*'s air group was dedicated to night operations and it played no role in the series of attacks launched during the day. At 0910hrs, TG 38.2 opened the largest air–sea battle in history up to that point with the launch of its first strike.

After being spotted by USN carrier aircraft, Kurita ordered his formation to increase speed to 24 knots and prepare for air attack. When no attack developed, the formation reduced speed and resumed zigzagging. A series of radar contacts on aircraft were reported over the next two hours. At 1000hrs a radar contact was gained on a large formation to the east. At 1025hrs, aircraft were sighted to the south. This was TG 38.2's first strike of the day. It was comprised of 45 aircraft—21 Hellcats, 12 Helldivers, and 12 Avengers. Most came from *Intrepid*, with ten Hellcats and four Avengers from *Cabot*. Commander William E. Ellis, the commander of *Intrepid*'s air group, led the combined strike.

The lead group of Japanese ships included the huge *Yamato* and *Musashi*. Of these two, *Musashi* was nearest, so Ellis selected her as the main target. He split the 12 Helldivers into two six-aircraft divisions to attack both battleships with their 1,000lb bombs. The two nearest large ships were the subject of the

The remnants of the First Diversion Attack Force fled north toward San Bernardino Strait following the Battle off Samar. The photo of Kurita's force was taken by an aircraft from *Hornet* on October 25 off Samar. At the center of the image is *Yamato*; to the left are *Nagato* and *Haguro*; light cruiser *Noshiro* is on the right. Despite two large strikes by TG 38.1 during the day, none of Kurita's ships received significant damage.

First Diversion Attack Force, 1030hrs October 24, 1944

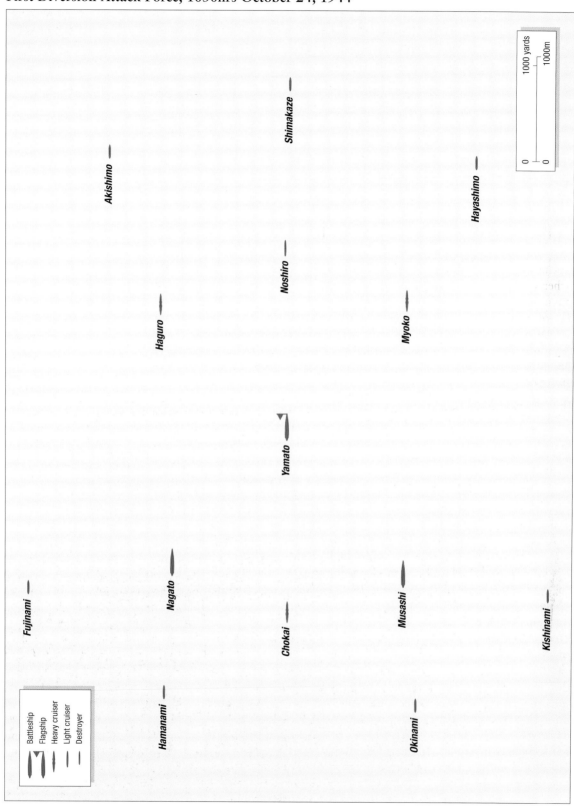

Shimakaze

Akishimo

Hayashimo

Noshiro

Haguro

Myoko

Yamato

Nagato

Fujinami

Chokai

Musashi

Kishinami

Hamanami

Okinami

0   1000 yards

0   1000m

Battleship
Flagship
Heavy cruiser
Light cruiser
Destroyer

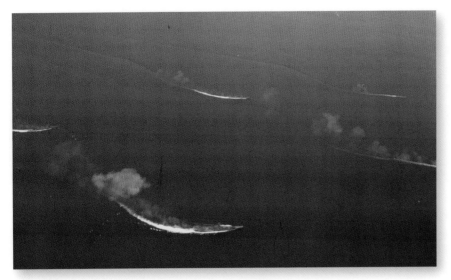

Kurita's fleet photographed maneuvering under attack during one of the first two American raids on October 24. The photograph was taken from a Helldiver from *Intrepid*. In the foreground is either *Musashi* or *Yamato*; in the background are two cruisers and a destroyer.

Avengers' attack. Two were ordered to go after heavy cruiser *Myoko* and the other six were directed against *Musashi*. These were divided into two three-plane sections in order to execute an anvil attack. The four Avengers from *Cabot* were allocated against *Yamato* in the center of the formation.

American pilots all remarked on the ferocity of the antiaircraft fire from the multi-colored 5in. bursts to the streams of tracers from the 25mm guns. The Japanese also used Type 3 incendiary shells from 18.1in. and 16in. main battery guns. Despite the spectacular appearances of this barrage, Japanese antiaircraft fire was generally ineffective. The giant Type 3 shells proved totally ineffective, and Japanese records indicate that the battleships fired a relatively low number of 6in. and 5in. shells during each attack, indicating that the fire-control systems were taking too long to generate a targeting solution. These and the ubiquitous 25mm guns damaged many aircraft, but of the over 250 aircraft that attacked during the day, only 18 were shot down. Though the numbers confirm the ineffectiveness of IJN antiaircraft fire, the American aviators displayed great courage pressing home their attacks through what was described as an impenetrable wall of flak.

For most of the day, *Musashi* was the center of attention. The first six Helldivers could only score several near misses. None had any real effect. As the vulnerable Avengers made their runs, Hellcats strafed the battleship along her length. At 1030hrs, the first important blow of the battle was recorded. An Avenger placed one torpedo amidships slightly abaft the bridge on *Musashi*'s starboard side. Due to a fault in the design of her side belt, slow flooding entered the adjacent boiler room. The effect of some 3,000 tons of water

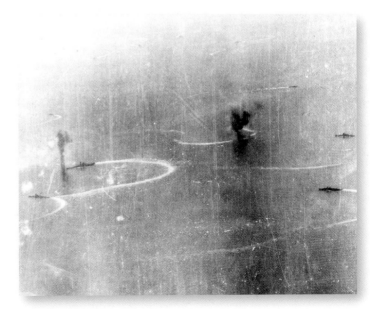

A Japanese battleship (at left either *Yamato* or *Musashi*) and other warships maneuver while under attack by USN carrier planes in the Sibuyan Sea. The ships in the lower left and the two at the extreme right are heavy cruisers. Note the use of a circular evasion maneuver, which was the IJN's standard tactic.

MUSASHI UNDER ATTACK (PP. 50–51)

The first air attack against the First Diversion Attack Force was mounted by aircraft from TG 38.1. The strike was led by Commander William E. Ellis of *Intrepid*'s air group, who selected *Musashi* as the focus of his attack. Six Helldivers began the attack. Flying into what was described as a seeming wall of antiaircraft fire, the Helldivers could only mange several near misses. Next up were the Avengers. Of the eight *Intrepid* Avengers, six were directed against *Musashi*. Per doctrine, these were divided into two three-plane sections for an anvil attack. Shown here are two of the three aircraft that attacked *Musashi* from her starboard side.

Flying over an escorting destroyer, one of the three aircraft was shot down by 5in. antiaircraft fire (**1**) before it could launch its torpedo. The two remaining aircraft got their torpedoes in the water, and the one launched by the lead Avenger (**2**) hit *Musashi* (**3**) just abaft the ship's huge superstructure. Both aircraft then went to full throttle and descended to an altitude of 200ft to exit the Japanese formation as quickly as possible. The torpedo hit shown here did little damage but was the first of as many as 15 that struck *Musashi*. No ship could withstand such a pounding.

was a 5.5° list, which was quickly reduced to a single degree by pumps in the affected boiler room and counterflooding on the opposite. Facing *Musashi*'s intact antiaircraft batteries, one Avenger was shot down before it launched its torpedo and a second went down after deploying its weapon.

The two Avengers that attacked *Myoko* were even more successful. At 1029hrs, one torpedo hit the heavy cruiser on her starboard side aft. Her propulsion system was damaged, and her top speed reduced to 15 knots. The cruiser fell astern of the formation. Kurita was forced to send her back to Singapore for repairs without destroyer escort. Since *Myoko* was the flagship of *Sentai* 5, at 1100hrs the commander transferred to cruiser *Haguro*. *Myoko* limped back to Singapore but was out of the war. Four of Kurita's heavy cruisers were out of the battle before they had a chance to engage an enemy ship. *Cabot*'s small group of torpedo aircraft attacked *Yamato*, but the battleship dodged all torpedoes directed at her.

Following the opening attack, the First Diversion Attack Force continued out of the Tablas Strait and into the Sibuyan Sea. It enjoyed only a brief respite from air attack. The second American strike, also from *Intrepid* and *Cabot*, was launched at 1045hrs, detected by Japanese radar 50NM away, and then sighted by the Japanese at 1203hrs. This attack included 42 aircraft—19 Hellcats, 12 Helldivers, and 11 Avengers. The Japanese opened fire at 1207hrs and ceased fire only eight minutes later. In that short period, the well-coordinated assault inflicted more damage on *Musashi*. The new strike leader took the advice of Commander Ellis to concentrate solely on *Musashi*.

Again, Helldivers opened the attack. The 12 bombers scored at least two direct hits and five near misses. One 1,000lb hit forward and passed through *Musashi*'s bow without exploding. The second hit just to the port side of the stack and penetrated two decks before exploding. The resulting damage forced the abandonment of the port-side inboard engine room, which reduced the ship to three shafts. A fire near one of the boiler rooms was quickly extinguished. Adding to the chaos, *Musashi*'s steam siren was damaged, and it continued to sound off and on for the remainder of the action.

Once again *Intrepid*'s Avengers deployed to conduct an anvil attack. Of the nine aircraft, eight got their torpedoes in the water and headed toward the huge battleship. As was the case for the entire series of attacks, it is impossible to precisely trace the number of hits suffered by *Musashi*; American and Japanese records do not even coincide on the overall number of attacks during the day. It is probable that the second wave of Avengers put three torpedoes into *Musashi*'s port side. One hit near the stack on the junction of the outboard port engine room and the port hydraulic machinery space; it caused slow flooding but little else. Another hit forward of the armored citadel and caused massive flooding into several large spaces. The last confirmed hit occurred abaft Turret No. 2. Despite these three additional hits, *Musashi* remained on an even keel, but was noticeably down by the bow. In exchange, *Musashi* antiaircraft gunners forced one Avenger to ditch some 15 miles away and shot down two Helldivers. During this attack, Japanese records indicate nine Type 3 shells were fired. American pilots were impressed that they were engaged at 25,000–30,000 yards, but no aircraft were damaged.

After only two attacks, Kurita's situation was becoming increasingly serious. He had lost a cruiser, and damage to *Musashi* reduced her top speed.

MARINDUQUE

MAESTRO DE CAMPO

DOS HERMANAS

1

A

1026

1200

2

1207

B

1100

BANTON

1
2

1000

SIMARA

USN FORCES

A. Raid 1: 45 aircraft: 21 Hellcats, 12 Helldivers, and 12 Avengers. Of these, ten Hellcats and four Avengers came from *Cabot*, the remainder from *Intrepid*.

B. Raid 2: 42 aircraft: 19 Hellcats, 12 Helldivers, and 11 Avengers from *Intrepid* and *Cabot*.

C. Raid 3: 68 aircraft: 16 Hellcats, 20 Helldivers, and 32 Avengers from *Essex* and *Lexington*.

D. Raid 4: 65 aircraft: 26 Hellcats, 21 Helldivers, and 18 Avengers. Of these, 12 Hellcats, nine Helldivers, and eight Avengers came from *Enterprise*, the rest from *Franklin*.

E. Raid 5: 31 aircraft: 16 Hellcats, 12 Helldivers, and three Avengers from *Intrepid* and *Cabot*.

TABLAS

ROMBLON

IJN FORCES

1. First Diversionary Attack Force, First Section
   Battleships: *Musashi, Yamato, Nagato*
   Heavy cruisers: *Myoko, Haguro, Chokai*
   Light cruiser: *Noshiro*
   Destroyers: *Shimakaze, Akishimo, Hayashimo, Kishinami, Okinami, Fujinami, Hamanami*
2. First Diversionary Attack Force, Second Section
   Battleships: *Haruna, Kongo*
   Heavy cruisers: *Chikuma, Kumano, Suzuya, Tone*
   Light cruiser: *Yahagi*
   Destroyers: *Kiyoshimo, Nowaki, Hamakaze, Isokaze, Urakaze, Yukikaze*
3. Battleship *Musashi*, destroyers *Shimakaze, Kiyoshimo*

Note: gridlines are shown at 10NM intervals.

SIBUY

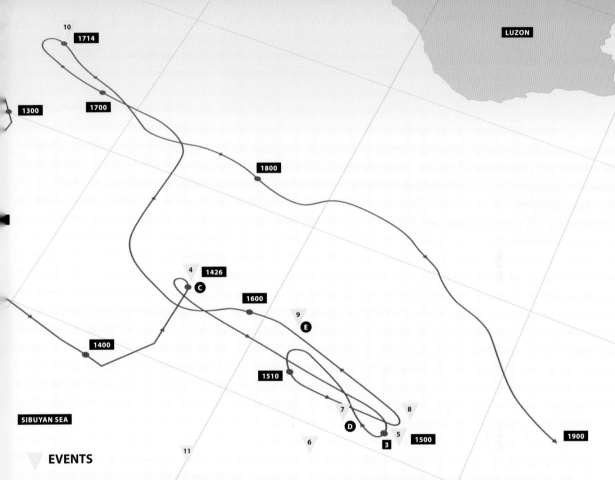

BATTLE OF THE SIBUYAN SEA

1026hrs–1920hrs, October 24, 1944

LUZON

SIBUYAN SEA

EVENTS

1. 1026hrs: Six Helldivers attack both *Musashi* and *Yamato*; no hits are scored. The six Avengers from *Intrepid* that attack *Musashi* score one torpedo hit but lose two aircraft. The last two *Intrepid* Avengers attack heavy cruiser *Myoko*; one torpedo hit reduces the ship's speed to 15 knots. *Myoko* is ordered to return, unescorted, to Singapore.

2. 1207hrs: The second strike from *Intrepid* and *Cabot* focuses on *Musashi*. The Helldivers attack first and score two hits and five near misses. The nine Avengers from *Intrepid* score three torpedo hits, reducing *Musashi*'s speed to 22 knots. The First Diversionary Attack Force is forced to reduce speed to allow *Musashi* to continue in formation. American losses in the attack are one Avenger and two Helldivers.

3. 1330hrs: Most of the strike aircraft from *Essex* and *Lexington* attack *Musashi*. The battleship takes four 1,000lb hits followed by three confirmed torpedo hits. *Musashi* goes down by the bow and her speed is reduced to 12 knots.

4. 1426hrs: Dive-bombers from *Essex* attack the other battleships of the First Section. *Yamato* is struck by three bombs forward, but her speed is unaffected. *Nagato* takes two bomb hits and suffers moderate damage to her secondary battery, but is able to remain in formation.

5. 1500hrs: *Musashi* is ordered to the west escorted by two destroyers.

6. 1510hrs: Aircraft from *Enterprise* and *Franklin* attack the crippled *Musashi*. The battleship is unable to maneuver and has only some 25 percent of its antiaircraft weapons operational. Dive-bombers score ten hits on *Musashi*, most forward and on the ship's massive superstructure. Avengers follow with four confirmed and four probable torpedo hits. *Musashi*'s speed is further reduced to 6 knots and she is unable to maneuver.

7. 1521hrs: *Haruna*, steaming with the Second Section, is attacked. She suffers five near misses, but her speed is unaffected.

8. 1530hrs: Kurita heads west to give other Japanese forces time to attack the Third Fleet.

9. Approximately 1550hrs: Aircraft from *Intrepid* and *Cabot* conduct their last attack, but probably score no hits.

10. 1714hrs: Kurita resumes course for San Bernardino Strait.

11. 1920hrs: *Musashi*'s crew is ordered to abandon ship; she sinks at 1936hrs.

Musashi was the center of American attentions and took 11 confirmed torpedoes and 16 bombs before sinking. In this image, she appears to have just been struck by a torpedo. The photo shows the difficulty aviators had in determining whether they conducted a successful attack or not. Note the relatively sparse antiaircraft fire above the formation.

The superbattleship's well-trained damage-control crews performed well and did so all day; despite taking four torpedoes, *Musashi* was not in any danger of sinking. Counterflooding reduced her buoyancy reserve, but the ship had only a small list to port. However, with only three shafts operational, her best speed was reduced to 22 knots. Kurita ordered a reduction to 20 knots so *Musashi* could regain her place in the formation. Kurita's real concern was his total lack of air cover and the almost certain prospect of additional air attacks. These fears were reflected in his 1315hrs message addressed to Ozawa and the Southwest Area Fleet: "We are being subjected to repeated enemy carrier-based air attacks. Advise immediately of contacts and attacks made by you on the enemy." Kurita would have been even more concerned had he known that neither Japanese force was able to mount significant attacks on TF 38 to relieve the pressure on his force.

Halsey had no intention of providing Kurita with a breathing space. At 1050hrs, TG 38.3 launched its only attack of the day. This totaled 58 aircraft from *Essex* and *Lexington*—16 Hellcats, 20 Helldivers, and 32 Avengers. This attack began at 1330hrs and was split between *Yamato* and *Musashi*. During the ensuing 20 minutes, *Musashi* was turned into a floating wreck.

Most aircraft went after *Musashi*. With her speed reduced and unable to fully maneuver, she was a much easier target. Despite the heavy fire directed against them, the Helldivers performed their mission of preparing the way for the torpedo bombers. At least four 1,000lb bombs hit *Musashi*. Three hits caused minimal damage as they impacted near the forward 18in. turret and exploded in the unoccupied crew accommodation spaces below. Damage from the final hit that exploded on contact when it hit the starboard side of the stack was not serious, but the explosion devastated many nearby 25mm triple mounts and caused heavy casualties among the gun crews.

While the Helldivers added to the topside carnage, damage from the Avengers was much more serious. Three more torpedo hits were confirmed in the third attack, bringing the total to seven. Two struck forward of the armored citadel on either side of the bow. The design flaw of having comparatively little compartmentation in the unarmored forward section of the ship led to massive flooding. In addition, the explosions forced the hull plating outward creating what looked like a huge plow throwing water up as the ship moved forward. Another torpedo struck the starboard side close to the previous starboard side hit. This increased flooding and forced the abandonment of the starboard hydraulic machinery room. A possible fourth hit was reported by some witnesses near the forward 6.1in. triple turret on the starboard side.

By the end of the third attack, *Musashi* was down by the bow after being hit by seven torpedoes. Throughout the day, *Musashi*'s damage-control crews did an excellent job keeping her on an even keel until she was literally pounded under the waves.

Damage from seven torpedo and six bomb hits would have proved fatal for any other battleship. But *Musashi* was in no immediate danger of sinking since there was no progressive flooding. Excellent damage control reduced the 2° list to starboard, but the original freeboard of 32.8ft on the bow was down to 19.6ft. Cumulative damage reduced the ship's top speed to 16 knots, and this was further reduced by the ship's captain to 12 knots for fear that *Musashi* could plunge by the bow. Since *Musashi* was unable to maintain formation, at 1500hrs Kurita ordered her to proceed to the west with destroyers *Shimakaze* and *Kiyoshimo*. *Tone* was also hit at 1330hrs with three bombs, two of which exploded. Damage was light, and neither the cruiser's speed nor fighting capabilities were impaired.

According to Japanese records, the fourth attack against the First Diversion Attack Force occurred between 1426hrs and 1450hrs. This attack

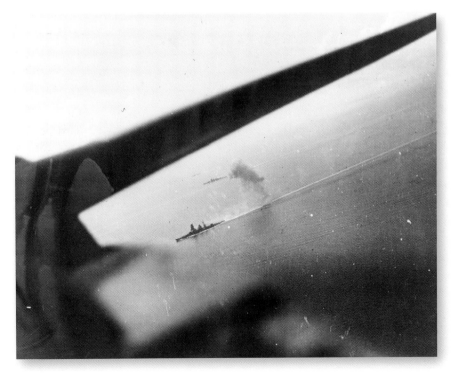

TG 38.2 launched the first two strikes against the First Diversion Attack Force on October 24. This is a photo taken by an *Intrepid* aircraft during one of these attacks. Battleship *Nagato* is in the foreground with heavy cruiser *Haguro* in the center of the image.

featured aircraft from *Essex*'s air group, at least 12 Helldivers and eight Hellcats. The dive-bombers passed up the crippled *Musashi* and went after the other two battleships in the First Section, *Yamato* and *Nagato*. At least three bombs hit *Yamato* forward. One penetrated the bow and exploded below the waterline. Flooding by 3,000 tons of seawater created a 5° list to port. Counterflooding reduced the list to 1°. *Yamato* was slightly down by the bow, but her speed was unaffected. The other two bombs hit near Turret No. 1 but neither caused significant damage. About the same time, *Nagato* was subjected to Helldiver attack. She was hit by two bombs and near-missed by three more. The bomb that struck the boat deck destroyed or damaged five 5.5in. casemate guns and jammed one of the Type 89 5in. dual-purpose mounts. Damage to one of the boiler room air intakes caused a temporary reduction of speed to 22 knots.

The fifth air attack of the day was the heaviest yet. It combined the first attack from TG 38.4 and the third attack of the day from TG 38.2. From TG 38.4, aircraft from *Enterprise* (12 Hellcats, nine Helldivers, and eight Avengers) and *Franklin* (14 Hellcats, 12 Helldivers, and ten Avengers) took off about 1315hrs. By the time the strike arrived in the area of the First Diversion Attack Force, Kurita had turned his main body to the west and *Musashi* was left by herself with only two destroyers. More than half of the strike went after the crippled battleship, with the other half attacking Kurita's main body.

Most of the aircraft attacking *Musashi* were from *Enterprise*. By this point, *Musashi* was unable to defend herself. She had a top speed of 12 knots and could not maneuver. Only about a quarter of her antiaircraft guns

Battleship *Nagato* in action during the Battle of the Sibuyan Sea. Two bombs have missed, and the battleship appears to have just fired some Type 3 *"sanshikidan"* shells from her 16in. forward guns. These were designed to engage aircraft, but their use was a serious matter since they could damage the linings of the gun barrels and affect accuracy. *Nagato* fired these special rounds in each of the first two American raids on October 25.

remained in action. While the Hellcats suppressed the escorting destroyers, the Helldiver and Avenger pilots pressed their attacks against the wallowing giant. The results against the near-defenseless battleship were devastating. Of the 18 Helldivers that dove on *Musashi*, 11 claimed hits. On this occasion, the aviators' claims were not inflated. Japanese sources agreed that within minutes, *Musashi* was pounded by ten 1,000lb bombs. This barrage can be detailed with some degree of certainty. One bomb hit forward of Turret No. 1 and added to the damage there from earlier bombs. Another bomb hit the roof of the same turret and failed to penetrate its thick roof armor. Another hit to the starboard side of the turret and penetrated two decks before exploding against the main armored deck. Two bombs hit together between the forward 6.1in. turret and the superstructure, exploded on contact, and did minimal damage. Another two hit just to port in the same general area, penetrated two decks, and exploded on the main armored deck without penetrating. The eighth bomb hit the port side of the massive superstructure and exploded on contact, causing devastation to nearby 25mm mounts and their crews. Another projectile hit the top of the superstructure and destroyed the main battery fire-control director and its rangefinder. The resulting explosion caused significant personnel casualties on the bridge and operations room totaling 78 killed and wounded. Among the wounded was the ship's captain. The final hit landed abaft the superstructure but caused only minor damage.

Musashi was equally helpless against the Avengers. The eight *Enterprise* Avengers conducted an anvil attack, and all claimed hits. At this point in the action, the accounts of *Musashi*'s surviving crewmembers are not reliable. It is certain that four more torpedoes hit the ship. The first was on the port side in the area of the magazine for Turret No. 1. Another hit on the port side was recorded abeam the superstructure, flooding one boiler room. The

Another image of the First Diversion Attack Force under attack on October 24. The large ship to the left is probably *Nagato*, making the light cruiser in the right foreground *Noshiro*.

third hit to port was placed just aft of the stack. It was in the same area of an earlier hit, and it immediately flooded the outboard engine room. The only confirmed hit on the starboard side occurred in the area of Turret No. 2. On top of the four confirmed hits, some Japanese accounts mention as many as six more. Two of these struck amidships on the port side but did not explode. All attacking aircraft returned safely, confirming the ineffectiveness of *Musashi*'s defenses at this point.

For the first time during the day, the Second Section built around battleships *Haruna* and *Kongo* came under attack. Helldivers selected *Haruna* for attack; five scored near misses at 1521hrs, but the ship's speed was not affected.

On the heels of TG 38.4's strike, aircraft from *Intrepid* and *Cabot* made their third attack of the day. Led by Commander Ellis flying his second mission, it included 16 Hellcats, 12 Helldivers, and the last three operational Avengers from *Intrepid*'s torpedo squadron. One of the Avengers claimed a hit on *Musashi*'s stern, but this is not supported by Japanese accounts. Flying their second sortie of the day, the Helldiver pilots must have been fatigued. They did not score a hit.

Following the last air attack of the day, Kurita took stock of the day's action. After taking a minimum 16 bomb and at least 11 and probably 15 torpedo hits, it was certain that *Musashi* was doomed. Her list increased to 10–12° and her bow was down by another 6½ft. With only the starboard shafts still operational, top speed was reduced to 6 knots. At 1715hrs, Kurita ordered *Musashi* to beach herself on nearby Sibuyan Island. It was too late—*Musashi* could barely move on her last operational shaft and the flooding continued unchecked. Severely down by the bow, the ship would not answer to her helm and so circled slowly. By 1800hrs, the last boiler room was abandoned due to flooding, leaving the ship without power.

Musashi's demise was now only minutes away. By 1900hrs, the list increased to 15°; by 1920hrs, the list reached 30°. The bow continued to sink, and the sea reached the port side of Turret No. 1. Finally, the order to abandon ship was given. Minutes after the order was issued, *Musashi*'s stern rose as the bow sunk deeper, and then she began a slow roll to port. At 1936hrs, the ship turned bottom up and then slid under bow first. Three destroyers picked 1,376 survivors from the water, but another 1,023 were lost. *Musashi* became the largest ship ever sunk by air attack.

The attacks on the First Diversion Attack Force on October 24, 1944 represented the largest air–sea battle in history up to that point. Kurita's force was subjected to a series of attacks by over 250 carrier aircraft. For the loss of 18 aircraft, the Americans sank *Musashi*, torpedoed heavy cruiser *Myoko* and forced her back to base, and inflicted varying degrees of damage on three other battleships. Despite this pounding, the First Diversion Attack Force had survived in better condition than could have been expected. The 250 sorties mounted by TF 38 brought a relatively weak return. This was due to the over-concentration on a single target—*Musashi*. With no single attack coordinator, each of the American carrier air groups was drawn to the largest target available, and the temptation proved irresistible after *Musashi* was left crippled and looked easy to finish off. The overall effect was that while *Musashi* acted as a torpedo and bomb sponge, the other primary ships of the First Diversion Attack Force suffered little damage.

The over-concentration on *Musashi* did not stop TF 38's aviators from claiming a much greater success. They reported that both Yamato-class battleships had been crippled with one probably sunk, *Nagato* was hit and badly damaged, and a Kongo-class battleship was crippled. Four heavy cruisers,

Heavy cruiser *Haguro* or *Myoko* firing at attacking USN carrier planes during one of the five air attacks against the First Diversion Attack Force mounted by TF 38. The heavy smoke is from the 25mm guns, exhibiting one of the weaknesses of this weapon.

two light cruisers, and six destroyers were reported sunk or damaged. If true, the First Diversion Attack Force had been rendered combat ineffective. This false assessment led to the most dramatic phase of the Battle of Leyte Gulf.

KURITA'S INDECISION

As *Musashi* struggled to stay afloat, Kurita began to doubt his prospects for success. To him, it appeared the First Diversion Attack Force was fighting the Americans by itself. The weight of air attack had increased throughout the day indicating that Japanese land-based air forces had been unable to accomplish their mission of neutralizing Halsey's carriers. No communication had been received from Ozawa, so it was unclear if his force had successfully attacked the Third Fleet or lured it north. Given his situation, at 1530hrs Kurita ordered his force to change course to the west, away from San Bernardino Strait. Delaying his advance would lessen the pressure from air attack and give time for Japanese air attacks to achieve better results, Kurita assessed. He sent a message to Toyoda at 1600hrs explaining his rationale. After briefly heading north, he changed course again at 1714hrs back toward San Bernardino Strait since no more air attacks had been suffered since about 1550hrs. It took Toyoda until 1813hrs to respond with "All forces will dash to the attack trusting in divine assistance." This terse response was received on *Yamato* at 1915hrs after Kurita had already resumed his advance.

Kurita adjusted his plans in the aftermath of his delayed advance toward Leyte Gulf. At 2145hrs, he sent a message with his new timetable. The reduced but still potent First Diversion Attack Force with its four battleships, six heavy cruisers, two light cruisers, and 11 destroyers would transit San Bernardino Strait at 0100hrs on October 25, head down the east coast of Samar, and arrive at Leyte Gulf at about 1100hrs.

Yamato photographed under attack on October 24. Note that the wooden deck has been darkened in preparation for a night battle exiting San Bernardino Strait.

Unknown to Kurita, TF 38 had finally located Ozawa's carriers at 1640hrs. With Kurita's force reported to be crippled, Halsey made the decision to take his entire force north to attack and annihilate Ozawa's force on October 25 (a detailed examination of this controversial decision will be made in the second Campaign series volume on Leyte Gulf). This left San Bernardino Strait completely unguarded, and even unwatched. The First Diversion Attack Force approached the strait at 20 knots and went to general quarters, expecting a fight to force it. As the Japanese passed through on a clear night, no contact with any USN unit was made. After entering the Philippine Sea at 0037hrs, Kurita changed course to the south and headed to Leyte Gulf.

THE BATTLE OFF SAMAR

Few battles in the Pacific War featured forces seemingly as mismatched as those involved in what became known as the Battle off Samar. Yet few battles are as poorly understood. What resulted was an American victory against what seemed impossible odds. Though undeniably an example of the tenacity and bravery of the American sailor, it was also another example of the weakness of *Sho-1*.

On the morning of October 25, the three escort carrier groups of TG 77.4 under the command of Rear Admiral Thomas L. Sprague were operating east of Leyte. Two escort carriers were detached the day before, leaving 16; aboard these were some 480 aircraft—the equivalent of five Essex-class fleet carriers. The escort carriers were protected by nine destroyers and 12 destroyer escorts.

Neither side expected an encounter off Samar. Beginning at 0530hrs, the three escort carrier groups began to operate aircraft in the usual pattern of CAP, antisubmarine, and search missions. Each escort carrier group was known as "Taffy" after their radio call sign. Taffy 3 (TU 77.4.3) was the furthest north, operating off Samar; Taffy 2 (TU 77.4.2) was in the center position off the entrance to Leyte Gulf; and Taffy 1 (TU 77.4.1) was the furthest south off northern Samar. At 0645hrs, a series of reports indicated something strange to the north of Taffy 3. These were hard to explain since it was impossible for any Japanese force to be in the area. An Avenger from *Kadashan Bay* reported a force of four battleships, with eight cruisers and numerous destroyers at 0647hrs just 20NM north of Taffy 3. The pilot attacked one of the cruisers and reported being fired upon. When lookouts on Taffy 3 reported Japanese battleships and heavy cruisers to the north, there could be no more doubt. The battle began in earnest when shell splashes appeared astern of Taffy 3 at 0659hrs.

As surprised as Rear Admiral Clifton Sprague and the rest of the officers and men aboard Taffy 3 were, the Japanese were equally surprised. The first indication that Kurita received of the impending fight was at 0644hrs when a lookout on *Yamato* reported ships to the southeast. For reasons still difficult to understand, the Japanese never correctly identified the types of ships they were facing. No observers recognized the carriers as escort carriers. Instead, the Japanese saw fleet carriers. The escorting Fletcher-class destroyers and Butler-class destroyer escorts were identified as heavy cruisers and even battleships. Even as the battle developed, the Japanese never figured out the real nature of the force they were facing. This failure was one of the primary reasons the battle ended as it did.

Kurita's initial orders increased the confusion generated by the first contact at 0644hrs. He ordered "General Attack" at 0703hrs, meaning that each ship or division proceeded on its own against the Americans. This tactic abandoned any pretense of coordination between the various elements of the First Diversion Attack Force. Battleships *Yamato* and *Nagato* remained together, but *Kongo* and *Haruna* operated individually. For most of the engagement, the six heavy cruisers operated in three groups of two. The two destroyer flotillas, each led by a light cruiser, were kept to the rear by Kurita. This precluded them from screening the heavy ships and kept them out of position to make a torpedo attack. The General Attack decision was a critical error. It resulted in a loss of control by Kurita and a melee for the next two hours. His rationale for ordering an immediate, but uncoordinated, attack was to close the range as quickly as possible and knock out the carriers' flight decks. Throughout the battle, Kurita maneuvered to keep the weather gauge; by so doing, he could prevent the carriers from turning into the wind to conduct flight operations.

As Kurita gave orders that guaranteed he would have little control of the battle, Sprague on *Fanshaw Bay* began to fight a brilliant action. His first decisions were to order Taffy 3 to the east. He increased speed to 16 knots and then to 17.5 knots. Every available aircraft was ordered into the air at 0655hrs. Fortunately for Sprague, the wind was blowing generally from the east, allowing him to launch and recover aircraft while still moving away from the Japanese. Every ship was ordered to lay smoke. The Americans were fortunate that the humid air kept the smoke just above the surface of the sea, increasing the concealment of the ships behind it. There were also squalls in the area that would prove useful to Sprague. Under no illusion about his predicament, at 0701hrs Sprague began sending clear text messages reporting his situation and asking for help.

The battle opens

Sprague's best hope was to delay the Japanese until help arrived. The nearest help was Taffy 2 just to the south and Taffy 3 130NM away. The Seventh Fleet's battle line had just completed the annihilation of the First Diversion Attack Force's Third Section at the Battle of Surigao Strait that morning. When the battle began, the battle line under Rear Admiral Jessie Oldendorf was some 100NM miles away. To buy time, Taffy 3 deployed smoke and subjected Kurita's ships to constant air attack to delay their advance. Taffy 2's aircraft were also ordered to attack the Japanese; in fact, most of the sorties against Kurita's force during the action were flown by Taffy 2.

Kurita's cruisers possessed a marked speed advantage over Sprague's force. They moved to the north of Taffy 3, forcing it to the southwest. This was fine with Sprague since it put him on course to Leyte Gulf and nearer possible help from Oldendorf. The opening portion of the battle featured long-range Japanese battleship gunnery trying to find the range of the escort carriers. Beginning at 0659hrs, the salvos increased in frequency and gradually in accuracy. This growing pressure was alleviated when Sprague steered his force into a rain squall from 0706hrs until 0715hrs. Once out of the squall, Sprague changed course to the south, toward any help coming up from Leyte Gulf.

First Diversion Attack Force and Taffy 3, 0655hrs October 25, 1944

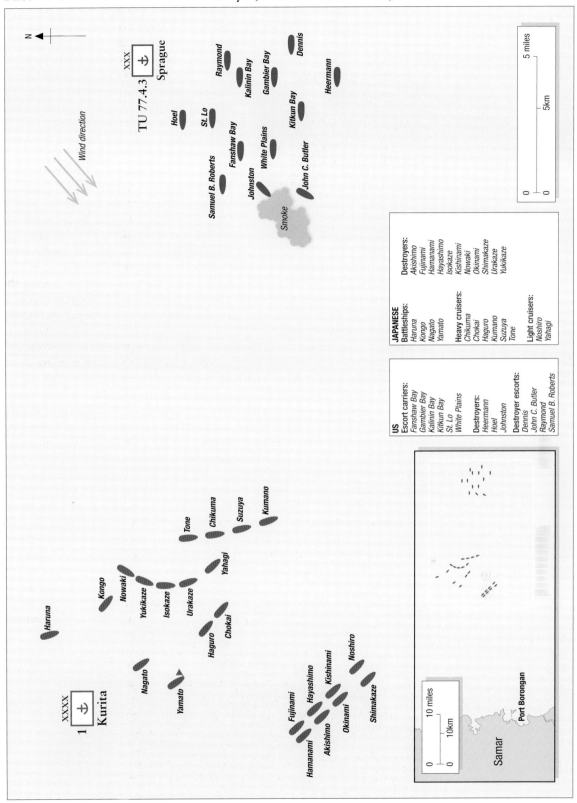

US

Escort carriers:
Fanshaw Bay
Gambier Bay
Kalinin Bay
Kitkun Bay
St. Lo
White Plains

Destroyers:
Heermann
Hoel
Johnston

Destroyer escorts:
Dennis
John C. Butler
Raymond
Samuel B. Roberts

JAPANESE

Battleships:
Haruna
Kongo
Nagato
Yamato

Heavy cruisers:
Chikuma
Chokai
Haguro
Kumano
Suzuya
Tone

Light cruisers:
Noshiro
Yahagi

Destroyers:
Akishimo
Fujinami
Hamanami
Hayashimo
Isokaze
Kishinami
Nowaki
Okinami
Shimakaze
Urakaze
Yukikaze

Sprague had a clear idea what he was doing; Kurita did not. When Sprague changed course to the south, Kurita had a chance to cut the distance by heading right for the Americans. Instead, most of his ships continued east before heading south. This opened the range on Sprague's carriers. Japanese gunnery was dependent on good visibility since, unlike USN gunnery that was directed by radar, Japanese radar was not good enough to direct fire. The rain and smoke affected the accuracy of Japanese gunnery throughout the battle and often forced the Japanese to temporarily cease fire.

Effective use of smoke was a key factor in Taffy 3's escape. In this photograph taken from *Kalinin Bay*, a destroyer escort and a Fletcher-class destroyer race out in front of *Gambier Bay* to lay smoke early in the engagement. USN ships could deploy heavy black smoke from their stacks and white chemical smoke from smoke generators. The humid conditions caused the smoke to combine and linger on the surface of the water. Heavy smoke greatly decreased the accuracy of Japanese gunnery.

Adding to Kurita's troubles was the counterattack of American destroyers. Taffy 3 had three destroyers, all Fletcher-class units with five 5in. guns and ten torpedoes. At 0716hrs, Sprague ordered them to conduct a torpedo counterattack to cover the escort carriers as they emerged from the squall. The actions of these destroyers formed another factor in saving the escort carriers from destruction.

Johnston, under Commander Ernest E. Evans, was nearest the Japanese cruisers and needed no orders to attack. Charging through a barrage of different-color geysers from Japanese shells (each Japanese ship had placed a different color dye in her shells to better determine their fall of shot), *Johnston* engaged *Kumano* with some 200 rounds of 5in. shells, of which several were observed to hit. Under fire from several Japanese heavy cruisers, Evans maintained course toward *Kumano* at 25 knots to make a torpedo attack. When within 10,000 yards, he unleashed all ten of his torpedoes. At 0727hrs, one of these struck *Kumano* and tore off a section of the cruiser's bow. Unable to maintain speed, *Kumano* was out of the battle. Vice Admiral Kazutaka Shiraishi, commander of *Sentai* 7, transferred with his staff to *Suzuya*. *Kumano* was ordered to limp back to San Bernardino Strait.

Sprague made good use of the three fleet destroyers attached to Taffy 3. The most aggressive was *Johnston*. Early in the battle she torpedoed heavy cruiser *Kumano*, knocking her out of the battle, as well as heavy cruiser *Suzuya* sent to her aid, and late in the battle she made a group of Japanese destroyers led by a light cruiser launch their torpedoes prematurely. This is *Johnston* on October 27, 1943, the day she was commissioned.

Kurita was down to five heavy cruisers, and *Suzuya* never got back into the fight after embarking Shiraishi.

It was inevitable that Evans would pay a price for approaching so close to a collection of enemy cruisers and battleships. This came at 0730hrs in the form of three large shells (possibly fired from *Yamato*) and a number of smaller shells that struck *Johnston*. The armor-piercing shells failed to explode, but damage was extensive. The aft machinery room was destroyed, which reduced speed to 17 knots. Most of the 5in./38 guns were knocked out, but after repairs were made during a providential 10-minute respite as a squall passed over, three were brought back online.

Johnston's commanding officer was Lieutenant-Commander Ernest E. Evans. For his actions on October 25, 1944, he was awarded the Medal of Honor. His exact fate remains unknown, but what is known is that he was not among those rescued after *Johnston* sank, making the award posthumous. Evans is shown here at *Johnston's* commissioning ceremonies in Seattle, Washington, in 1943.

While Evans dueled with Kurita's heavy cruisers, destroyer *Hoel* went after *Kongo*. She headed toward the 36,600-ton behemoth, opening fire with her 5in. guns at 14,000 yards, and then launched five torpedoes at 9,000 yards. *Kongo* evaded the torpedoes at 0733hrs, and her guns wreaked havoc on the destroyer, knocking out one engine, three 5in. guns, and the ship's radars. In response to an order from Sprague at 0742hrs to conduct a second torpedo attack, Commander Leon S. Kintberger went after heavy cruiser *Haguro* at 0750hrs. Getting to within 6,000 yards, he fired *Hoel's* last five torpedoes. These all missed. The final destroyer, *Heermann*, was on the far side of the formation and did not get Sprague's original order to conduct a torpedo attack. By the time *Hoel* conducted her second torpedo run against *Haguro*, *Heermann* joined the attack. At 0754hrs, *Heermann* launched seven torpedoes at *Haguro*, but these also missed. Next, *Heermann* spotted *Haruna*, and then Kurita's other three battleships off her port bow. Commander Amos T. Hathaway went after the lead target with his last three torpedoes. Despite the launch from only 4,400 yards at 0800hrs, none of the torpedoes scored. Amazingly, by using smoke and chasing shell splashes, *Heermann* was not hit by a single Japanese shell. Destroyer escort *Samuel B. Roberts* also joined the second torpedo attack. Using smoke, she got to within 4,000 yards of the Japanese heavy cruisers to launch her three torpedoes at 0752hrs. None found their target, but *Samuel B. Roberts* emerged from her experience unscathed by Japanese shellfire.

The first ship to succumb to the barrage of Japanese shellfire was the crippled *Hoel*. After her run against *Haguro*, and only able to make 17 knots, she was trapped between *Kongo* on one side and four heavy cruisers on the other. Using every possible method to evade the storm of shells directed against his ship, Kintberger survived for well over an hour after the first hit was recorded. *Hoel* took as many as 23 hits, but the actual number will never be known since most passed through the ship without exploding. The final engine was knocked out at 0830hrs, bringing the ship to a halt. Still under fire as the crew abandoned ship, *Hoel* rolled over at 0855hrs.

In addition to *Samuel B. Roberts*, the other destroyer escorts now entered the fray. These ships were not designed for engaging surface targets but for antisubmarine warfare. Each ship carried only three torpedoes and two

Battle off Samar: The situation at 0730hrs October 25, 1944

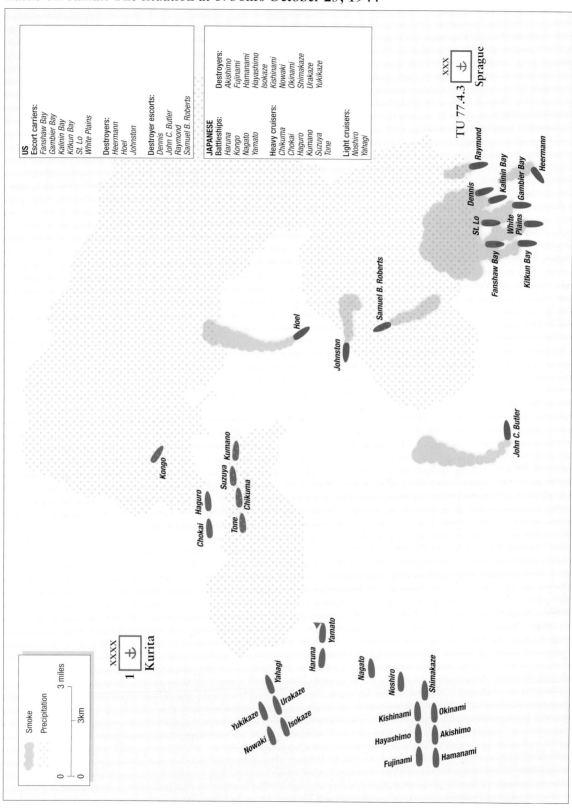

US

Escort carriers:
Fanshaw Bay
Gambier Bay
Kalinin Bay
Kitkun Bay
St. Lo
White Plains

Destroyers:
Heermann
Hoel
Johnston

Destroyer escorts:
Dennis
John C. Butler
Raymond
Samuel B. Roberts

JAPANESE

Battleships:
Haruna
Kongo
Nagato
Yamato

Heavy cruisers:
Chikuma
Chokai
Haguro
Kumano
Suzuya
Tone

Destroyers:
Akishimo
Fujinami
Hamanami
Hayashimo
Isokaze
Kishinami
Nowaki
Okinami
Shimakaze
Urakaze
Yukikaze

Light cruisers:
Noshiro
Yahagi

TU 77.4.3 — Sprague

Kurita

Smoke

Precipitation

0   3km

0   3 miles

This is the last photograph of *Samuel B. Roberts* taken a week or two before she was lost in the Battle off Samar on October 25, 1944.

5in. guns. *Raymond* answered Sprague's second call for a torpedo attack and used her three torpedoes to attack *Haguro* at 0756hrs. Launched from 6,000 yards, they were evaded. *Dennis* also selected a cruiser for her torpedo attack. From 8,000 yards, she fired her three torpedoes at *Tone*; again, all missed. Both *Raymond* and *Dennis* were undamaged by the storm of 8in. shells directed against them.

John C. Butler was the last destroyer escort to get into the action. In response to an order from Sprague at 0826hrs for the destroyer escorts on the starboard side of the formation to get between the carriers and the Japanese heavy cruisers on their port quarter, *John C. Butler* and *Dennis* took the cruisers under gunfire. *John C. Butler* sought an opportunity to use her torpedoes but was unable to close the range on the Japanese cruisers. By this time, *Chikuma* and *Tone* were the lead cruisers. The destroyer escorts were at least able to distract the cruisers' gunfire; at 0850hrs, *Dennis* received the first of two hits, but the damage was minor and her speed was unaffected. *Samuel B. Roberts* also was struck at 0850hrs. At 0900hrs, the destroyer escort was hit by two or three 14in. shells from *Kongo*. The large shells tore a huge hole in the side of the ship and knocked out all power. A total of six shells hit the ship. This prompted an order to abandon ship at 0910hrs for the crew of 178. Half (89 of them) did not survive. *Samuel B. Roberts* sank at 1005hrs.

Up until this point, the Japanese destroyers had played no part in the battle. Apparently on his own initiative, at 0845hrs Rear Admiral Masatomi Kimura, commander of the 10th Torpedo Flotilla, ordered his ships to make a torpedo attack. Led by light cruiser *Yahagi*, Kimura's

Of the three destroyers assigned to Taffy 3, only *Heermann* survived the battle. This is *Heermann* laying an effective smoke screen early in the battle as seen from *Kalinin Bay*.

JOHNSTON'S EPIC CHARGE (PP. 70–71)

Of the three Fletcher-class destroyers assigned to Taffy 3, *Johnston* (**1**) was the most aggressive and effective on October 25. Under the command of Commander Ernest E. Evans, *Johnston* performed brilliantly from the start of the Battle off Samar until its final stages.

When the Japanese fleet was sighted, Evans brought his crew to General Quarters and prepared for action. His ship was the first to engage the Japanese cruisers at 0710hrs when he unleashed a barrage of 5in. shells from a distance of 18,000 yards. *Johnston* immediately began laying smoke to hide the escort carriers of Taffy 3. After Taffy 3 emerged from a squall, Admiral Sprague ordered his destroyers to conduct a covering torpedo attack. *Johnston* was the first to respond, and Evans selected the nearest target, a column of four Japanese heavy cruisers led by *Kumano* (**2**).

Charging at 25 knots, *Johnston* headed for the cruisers. Evans brought *Kumano* under fire with his 5in. battery (**3**). Over 200 rounds were fired, and some were observed to have hit the cruiser. Each of the four cruisers targeted the American destroyer with their 8in. guns. A forest of shell splashes (**4**) soon rose around

Johnston. There were different colors evident in the columns of water reflecting the dye each cruiser used to spot its fall of shot. In spite of the volume of fire, *Johnston* was untouched.

When Evans got to within 10,000 yards of *Kumano*, he emptied all ten of his torpedo tubes at the cruiser. One of these hit *Kumano*'s bow at 0727hrs; with her speed reduced, she was forced out of the battle, which was an important contribution this early in the action. To compound matters, heavy cruiser *Suzuya* was ordered to pick up the commander of *Sentai* 7 aboard *Kumano*. This and the fact that she was already damaged from air attack that reduced her speed to 20 knots meant she was also effectively out of the battle.

Following her torpedo attack, *Johnston* headed back toward Taffy 3 under cover of her own smoke. Her brave attack proved costly since at about 0730hrs she was struck by three large shells and then three smaller ones that caused heavy damage. Under almost constant gunfire, she finally went down at 1010hrs.

On April 1, 2021, wreckage found at 21,180ft (the deepest debris ever found) was confirmed as that of *Johnston*.

flagship and four destroyers closed on the carriers until they were 10,500 yards astern of *Kalinin Bay*. *Johnston* spotted this new threat and charged out of the smoke. Evans engaged *Yahagi* with gunfire at 7,000 yards, and several hits were gained. Then Evans engaged the next destroyer in column, again claiming several hits. Kimura ordered his torpedoes fired from about 10,500 yards—not an ideal range for even the formidable Type 93. *Yahagi* launched seven torpedoes at 0905hrs, followed by three destroyers beginning at 0915hrs (*Urakaze* fired four, *Isokaze* eight, and *Yukikaze* four). No hits were scored, though Kimura claimed three carriers and a cruiser sunk. This was the largest Japanese torpedo barrage of the battle (*Haguro* and *Tone* had earlier fired eight and nine, respectively). Torpedo combat was a critical part of Japanese doctrine; the failure to gain even a single torpedo hit during the battle speaks of the failure of Japanese command and control and was another reason for their defeat.

Evans may have been responsible for Kimura's premature torpedo attack, but now his ship was about to pay the ultimate price. The Japanese destroyers and *Yahagi* took *Johnston* under fire, joined by as many as three heavy cruisers. The hits began to pile up. By 0920hrs, Evans was reduced to conning the ship by yelling orders through an open hatch on the fantail to men below turning the rudder manually. At 0945hrs, Evans finally gave the order to abandon ship. The Japanese destroyers closed in and continued to pound the wreck. After an epic fight, *Johnston* rolled over and sank at 1010hrs. Most of the crew of 327 got into the water, but 186, including Evans, were lost.

The ordeal of the escort carriers

As effective as the American destroyers and, to a lesser extent, destroyer escorts were in shielding the escort carriers from attack, Sprague's carriers were still the primary Japanese targets during the engagement. As such, they were subjected to a barrage of battleship and heavy cruiser gunfire for over two hours. Smoke screens laid by the American ships were generally effective in keeping the Japanese from getting a direct view to the carriers, but at times visibility was excellent with the carriers in full view.

Mighty *Yamato* opened fire at 0659hrs and fired four salvos by 0709hrs. Her third salvo straddled *White Plains*, with one of the shells striking the carrier and causing some underwater damage. Around 0800hrs, to evade torpedoes fired from *Hoel* aimed at *Haguro*, *Yamato* turned due north. This evasive maneuver forced her to the north for almost ten minutes until the torpedo tracks disappeared, placing her at the rear of Kurita's formation and effectively removing her from the battle for a period. *Nagato* opened fire at 0701hrs at a carrier assessed to be 36,000 yards away. After the three salvos, the battleship stopped firing having hit nothing.

Under fire from the battleships, Sprague's initial course was to the east-southeast at full speed—17.5 knots. As the Japanese heavy cruisers began to pressure his formation's port quarter, Sprague was forced to alter course to the southwest. *Kalinin Bay* was at the rear of the formation. She took a battleship shell at 0750hrs (probably from *Haruna*) that went through the hangar deck and out of her unarmored hull. As many as 14 other hits followed, all probably from 8in. shells. *Kalinin Bay* retaliated against the cruisers at 18,000 yards with her aft 5in./38 gun. The smoke generated from all six carriers and from the destroyers and destroyer escorts on their starboard

Battle off Samar: The situation at 0900hrs October 25, 1944

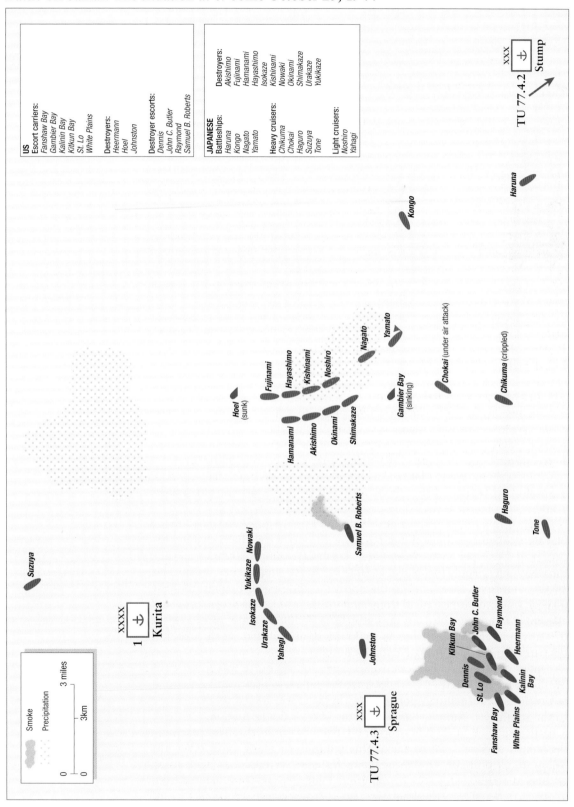

US
Escort carriers:
Fanshaw Bay
Gambier Bay
Kalinin Bay
Kitkun Bay
St. Lo
White Plains

Destroyers:
Heermann
Hoel
Johnston

Destroyer escorts:
Dennis
John C. Butler
Raymond
Samuel B. Roberts

JAPANESE
Battleships:
Haruna
Kongo
Nagato
Yamato

Heavy cruisers:
Chikuma
Chokai
Haguro
Suzuya
Tone

Light cruisers:
Noshiro
Yahagi

Destroyers:
Akishimo
Fujinami
Hamanami
Hayashimo
Isokaze
Kishinami
Nowaki
Okinami
Shimakaze
Urakaze
Yukikaze

TU 77.4.2 ⚓ Stump

Kongo

Haruna

Nagato

Yamato

Fujinami
Hayashimo
Kishinami
Noshiro

Chokai (under air attack)

Hoel (sunk)

Hamanami
Akishimo
Okinami
Shimakaze

Gambier Bay (sinking)

Chikuma (crippled)

Suzuya

Kurita XXXX ⚓ 1

Samuel B. Roberts

Haguro

Tone

Yukikaze Nowaki
Isokaze
Urakaze
Yahagi

Johnston

Kitkun Bay
John C. Butler
Raymond
Heermann
Dennis
St. Lo
Kalinin Bay

TU 77.4.3 Sprague XXX ⚓

Fanshaw Bay
White Plains

Smoke
Precipitation

3 miles
3km

0
0

74

Taken from an American aircraft, *Yamato* (right) steams in one direction while another battleship (left) steams in the opposite direction. This could show the aftermath of destroyer *Heermann's* torpedo salvo directed at *Haruna*; though the torpedoes missed, *Yamato* was forced to turn away and head north for 10NM until the torpedoes ran out of fuel.

quarter succeeded in hiding the carriers from direct Japanese observation for much of the battle. The Japanese shot slowly and methodically with four-gun salvos, allowing the escort carriers to chase salvos. The smoke and evasive maneuvering kept damage to a minimum, but of the six escort carriers, four were eventually hit. *Fanshaw Bay* took six 8in. hits, all forward, that killed three and wounded 20. *White Plains* took a probable 6in. hit and suffered light damage. *Kitkun Bay* was not hit but suffered several personnel casualties from near misses. *St. Lo* suffered no damage during the battle.

The Japanese cruisers continued to close the range to the escort carriers. *Gambier Bay* now took the brunt of Japanese attentions since she was at the rear of Sprague's formation. As early as 0741hrs, the escort carrier began using her 5in. gun to ward off the cruisers. For over 30 minutes, she chased salvos until the range fell to 10,000 yards. At 0810hrs, the inevitable happened when a shell struck the aft part of the flight deck and started a fire. *Chikuma* was probably responsible for the catastrophic hit at 0820hrs that wrecked the engine room, reducing speed to 11 knots, and forced *Gambier Bay* to fall behind the rest of the formation. *Yamato* rejoined the fight at 0822hrs, opening fire on the carrier. *Heermann* closed on the carrier at 0841hrs to find her burning and listing 20°. Continued Japanese fire resulted in more hits, with most of the armor-piercing shells passing through the ship. Hit by as many as 26 shells from *Yamato*, *Haruna*, and several cruisers, *Gambier Bay* went dead in the water at 0845hrs; five minutes later, the captain gave the order to abandon ship. *Gambier Bay* capsized at 0907hrs, one of only two carriers sunk by gunfire during the entire war.

Sprague had used every measure at his disposal to avoid annihilation. By about 0900hrs, the last two Japanese heavy cruisers, *Haguro* and *Tone*, were off his port beam at a range of 8,000 yards. Their fire was increasingly accurate. Even though his escorts had performed beyond all expectations, with three already sunk or sinking, at 0910hrs Sprague ordered his remaining escorts to make another attack. This attack never happened; *Tone* and *Haguro* ceased fire by 0917hrs, and minutes later the torpedoes from *Yahagi* and her destroyers began to appear around the carriers. None hit, but some exploded prematurely near the carriers. Sprague did not know that Kurita

Gambier Bay is straddled by Japanese shells and falls behind the rest of Taffy 3. Barely visible to the right is the silhouette of a Japanese heavy cruiser.

had called off the attack at 0911hrs with an order for his remaining ships to head north and join with flagship *Yamato*. At 0925hrs, one of the signalmen on Sprague's flagship confirmed the Japanese withdrawal with the immortal remark: "God damn it, boys, they're getting away!"

Escort carrier air attacks

Unrelenting American air attacks were the main reason for the Japanese defeat. Taffy aircrews were not highly trained for maritime attack, and torpedoes or armor-piercing bombs were in short supply. Most Avengers were launched with bombs instead of more effective torpedoes for two reasons. Torpedoes took more time and preparation to load, and the deck crews on Taffy 3 did not have the luxury of time. Also, once loaded with a heavy torpedo, the Avengers could only be launched if the escort carrier steamed into the wind. Moving downwind, like Taffy 3 was forced to do for most of the action, did not get enough wind across the flight deck.

At the beginning of the action, Taffy 3's carriers were ordered to launch all operational aircraft. *Kitkun Bay* launched 11 Wildcats and six Avengers shortly after 0700hrs. The commander of the ship's air group stayed aloft for eight hours acting as overall strike director. By 0730hrs, all operational aircraft were in the air. This included 51 Wildcats and 44 Avengers with an assortment of weapons, but only one carried a torpedo. Sprague ordered the first attacks against the heavy cruisers approaching off his port quarter. These early attacks reduced *Suzuya*'s speed and effectively forced her out of the battle. The last Taffy 3 strike was launched at 1015hrs with eight Avengers and two Wildcats.

The first attacks by Taffy 3 aircraft were conducted in groups of two or three with aircraft not properly armed for attacking ships. Because Taffy 3 could not steam into the wind while being pursued by Kurita's force, recovering aircraft during the battle was impossible. When they ran out of ordnance or fuel, they had to land on Taffy 2 or fly 100NM to the newly opened airfield at Tacloban. Even when lightly armed or unevenly unarmed, the aircraft made unceasing strafing runs in the case of the Wildcats or dummy bombing runs in the case of the Avengers. These attacks were poorly coordinated, but the Japanese, on the receiving end of incessant attacks, saw it differently. After the battle, Kurita and others commented that the attacks were well coordinated, skillful, and aggressive. The first properly coordinated strike did not occur until 0830hrs. Six Avengers and 20 Wildcats already airborne on various missions were joined with Taffy 2 aircraft for a large strike.

Taffy 2 contributed most aircraft sorties during the battle. Admiral Stump ordered his aviators to cripple as many Japanese ships as possible instead of focusing on one or two. The first of six strikes consisted of 15 Avengers with torpedoes and 20 Wildcats; the second launched at 0833hrs included 16 Avengers with torpedoes and eight Wildcats; the third mustered 12 Avengers (five with torpedoes) and eight Wildcats. The fourth, launched at 1115hrs, was the biggest of the day with 37 Avengers and 19 Wildcats. The fifth consisted of 11 Avengers (with the last three available torpedoes) and eight fighters launched at 1331hrs. The last strike, launched just after 1500hrs, included 26 Avengers and 24 Wildcats. Total ordnance used by Taffy 2 in these strikes included 49 torpedoes, 76 tons of bombs, and 276 rockets. Though it was operating just to the southeast of Taffy 3, the only time Taffy 2 came under fire was around 0854hrs when *Haruna*'s 14in. guns briefly fired on the three destroyers screening the rear of Taffy 2's formation.

Throughout the day, Japanese antiaircraft fire was heavy and fairly effective. Twelve Avengers and 11 Wildcats from Taffy 2 were shot down; losses from Taffy 3 are unknown but were likely to have been high.

The incessant attacks by the Taffy aircraft did more than just harass the Japanese. They were successful in sinking three heavy cruisers and

This photograph shows the effectiveness of American smoke screens on October 25. On the left a destroyer escort lays smoke that has nearly obscured an escort carrier behind. In the center of the image is a Fletcher-class destroyer laying smoke, and to the right is another escort carrier laying smoke. The three Japanese shell splashes are not close to any of these ships, nor to escort carrier *White Plains*, from which the photograph was taken.

Kitkun Bay prepares to launch FM-2 Wildcat fighters during the first 30 minutes of the engagement. In the distance, Japanese shells are splashing near *White Plains*.

damaging many other ships. The first real damage was to *Suzuya* when at 0735hrs she was attacked by about ten Avengers from Taffy 3. The Avengers managed a near miss aft that knocked out one of the propeller shafts, reducing speed to 20 knots. Another attack against *Suzuya* was mounted at 1050hrs by as many as 30 aircraft. This time, a near miss amidships turned deadly. Shrapnel from the bomb ignited the torpedoes in the starboard forward mount, igniting a fire that caused other torpedoes to explode at 1100hrs. The explosion caused extensive damage to the secondary battery and the machinery, which left the ship unmaneuverable. For a second time in the morning, Vice Admiral Shiraishi had to transfer, this time to *Tone*. The fires reached the remaining torpedoes, with a large explosion resulting at 1200hrs. In turn, this caused the magazine of the secondary battery to explode, and soon the entire ship was an inferno. Surviving crewmen were taken off by destroyer *Okinami* after the order to abandon ship was given at 1300hrs, and at 1320hrs *Suzuya* sank. Two-hundred forty-seven men were lost.

At 0825hrs, *Haguro* was hit by a bomb that penetrated the roof armor of Turret No. 2. The turret was knocked out, and 30 men were killed, but further damage was avoided by the quick closure of the antiflash doors leading to the magazine.

The saga of *Chokai* is hard to retrace since all her survivors were lost when destroyer *Fujinami* was sunk by TF 38 on October 27. Beginning at 0850hrs, *Chokai* was attacked by aircraft. At about 0905hrs, she was hit by 500lb bombs probably from Avengers from *Kitkun Bay*. Damage to the cruiser was severe: the forward engine rooms were knocked out and heavy fires took hold. Destroyer *Fujinami* was sent to her aid at 1018hrs; by then the cruiser was unmaneuverable, so the destroyer took the crew off and scuttled *Chokai* with torpedoes.

Chikuma was the last heavy cruiser to run foul of Taffy aircraft. A group of four Avengers from *Natoma Bay* from Taffy 2 attacked the cruiser at 0854hrs. One torpedo hit the cruiser and flooded both engine rooms. No repairs were possible, so when Kurita gave the order to break off the action at 0911hrs, *Chikuma*'s fate was sealed. Destroyer *Nowaki* was ordered to take off the crew and then scuttle her. This was accomplished at about 1100hrs. The fate of *Chikuma*'s crew was equally tragic as that of *Chokai*. After picking up the crew, *Nowaki* headed north toward San Bernardino Strait. Before she could escape, she was sunk by a force of Third Fleet light cruisers and destroyers early on October 26. Only a single member of *Chikuma*'s crew survived.

After Kurita broke off the action, Taffy aircraft continued to attack. At 1240hrs, *Kitkun Bay* Avengers attacked *Tone*. A single hit by a 500lb bomb temporarily affected the cruiser's steering gear, but she was able to escape. *Noshiro* was attacked at 1243hrs by aircraft from Taffy 2 and suffered minor damage from near misses.

Even without Taffy 1 contributing to the assault on the First Diversion Attack Force, the weight of air power directed at Kurita's force by the escort carriers has few parallels. Total escort carrier sorties on October 25 were 441—209 by Wildcats and 232 by Avengers. Sixty-eight of the Avengers carried torpedoes. This was more aircraft than TF 38 brought into action the previous day.

The Japanese view

Kurita was taken totally by surprise by the appearance of Taffy 3. He ordered his ships into a General Attack, which was usually used in a pursuit situation. Since the battle began as the Japanese were shifting from a night-cruising disposition to a circular formation for antiaircraft protection, there was additional confusion before Kurita could sort things out. American air attacks began almost immediately, and as already noted made an impression on the

Chikuma dead in the water after taking a torpedo hit that flooded her engine rooms. Note the extensive oil slick around the crippled cruiser. The destroyer standing by is *Nowaki*. The aircraft is an Avenger from *Kadashan Bay*. When Kurita issued his order to regroup, *Chikuma* could not comply, so *Nowaki* scuttled her and took off the crew.

USN FORCES

- **A.** Taffy 3 escort carriers
- **B.** Destroyer *Johnston*
- **C.** Destroyer *Hoel*
- **D.** Destroyer escort *Samuel B. Roberts*
- **E.** Destroyer *Heermann*
- **F.** Destroyer escort *Raymond*
- **G.** Destroyer escort *Dennis*
- **H.** Escort carrier *Gambier Bay*
- **I.** Three destroyers from Taffy 2
- **J.** Main body of Taffy 2

IJN FORCES

- **1.** *Sentai* 1: battleships *Yamato*, *Nagato*
- **2.** *Sentai* 3: battleship *Haruna*
- **3.** *Sentai* 3: Battleship *Kongo*
- **4.** *Sentai* 5: heavy cruisers *Haguro*, *Chokai*
- **5.** *Sentai* 7: heavy cruisers *Chikuma*, *Kumano*, *Suzuya*, *Tone*
- **6.** 10th Torpedo Flotilla: light cruiser *Yahagi*; destroyers *Nowaki*, *Isokaze*, *Urakaze*, *Yukikaze*
- **7.** 2nd Torpedo Flotilla: light cruiser *Noshiro*; destroyers *Shimakaze*, *Akishimo*, *Hayashimo*, *Kishinami*, *Okinami*, *Fujinami*, *Hamanami*

EVENTS

1. 0644hrs: A lookout from *Yamato* spots Taffy 3.

2. 0655hrs: Sprague orders Taffy 3 to head to the east.

3. 0659hrs: *Yamato* opens fire.

4. 0703hrs: Kurita orders "General Attack."

5. 0706hrs: Taffy 3 enters a squall.

6. 0716hrs: As Taffy 3 exits the squall, Sprague orders his destroyers to conduct a torpedo attack.

7. 0720hrs: *Johnston* fires ten torpedoes at *Kumano*.

8. 0723hrs: Sprague orders a course change to the southeast.

9. 0725hrs: *Hoel* fires five torpedoes at *Haruna*: is hit by shells from *Kongo*.

10. 0727hrs: *Kumano* is hit by a torpedo from *Johnston*.

11. 0730hrs: *Johnston* crippled by three battleship shells.

12. 0732hrs: Taffy 3 changes course to 170°; Sprague orders his aircraft to attack the Japanese cruisers.

13. 0735hrs: *Suzuya* hit by aircraft bombs; with speed reduced to 23 knots, she falls behind.

14. 0742hrs: Sprague issues second order to destroyers to conduct torpedo attack.

15. 0750hrs: *Kalinin Bay* hit.

16. 0750hrs: *Hoel* fires five remaining torpedoes at *Haguro*.

17. 0752hrs: *Samuel B. Roberts* fires her three torpedoes at Japanese cruisers.

18. 0754hrs: *Heerman* fires seven torpedoes at *Haguro*.

19. 0756hrs: *Raymond* fires her three torpedoes at *Haguro*.

20. 0759hrs: *Dennis* fires her three torpedoes at *Tone*.

21. 0800hrs: Taffy 3 steers south-southwest; *Gambier Bay* and *Kalinin Bay* become focus of Japanese gunfire.

22. 0810hrs: *Kongo* spots Taffy 2.

23. 0820hrs: *Gambier Bay* takes hit in machinery spaces from *Chikuma* and falls out of formation.

24. 0825hrs: *Haguro* hit by aircraft bomb.

25. 0841hrs: *Samuel B. Roberts* conducts gun duel with *Chikuma* after the cruiser closes on *Gambier Bay*.

26. 0854hrs: *Chikuma* torpedoed by aircraft from Taffy 2.

27. 0855hrs: *Hoel* sinks.

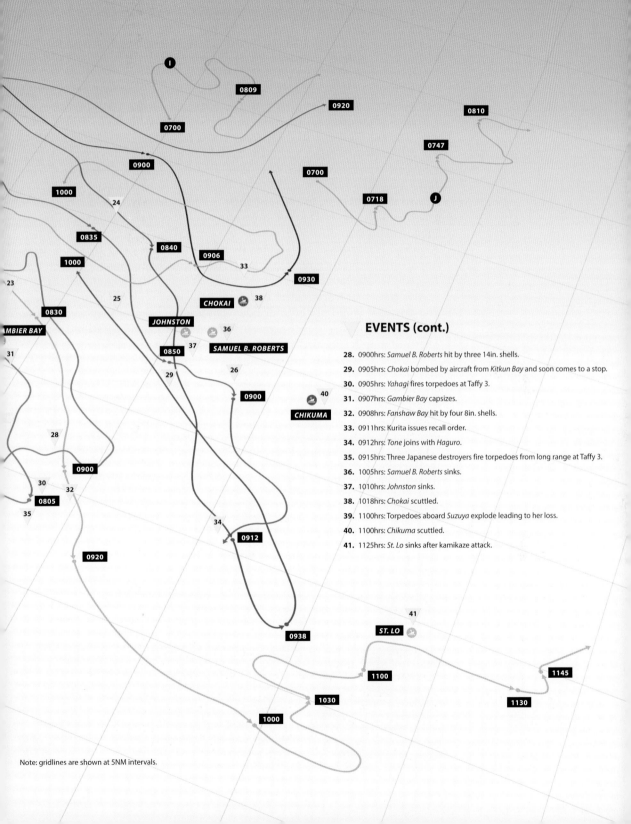

THE BATTLE OFF SAMAR

0644hrs–1125hrs October 25, 1944

I

0809

0920

0810

0700

0747

0900

0700

1000

0718

J

24

0835

0840

0906

1000

33

0830

0930

23

25

CHOKAI 38

MBIER BAY

JOHNSTON

36

31

37

0850

SAMUEL B. ROBERTS

29

26

0900

28

CHIKUMA 40

0900

30

34

32

35

0805

0912

0920

0938

ST. LO 41

1100

1145

1030

1130

1000

EVENTS (cont.)

28. 0900hrs: *Samuel B. Roberts* hit by three 14in. shells.

29. 0905hrs: *Chokai* bombed by aircraft from *Kitkun Bay* and soon comes to a stop.

30. 0905hrs: *Yahagi* fires torpedoes at Taffy 3.

31. 0907hrs: *Gambier Bay* capsizes.

32. 0908hrs: *Fanshaw Bay* hit by four 8in. shells.

33. 0911hrs: Kurita issues recall order.

34. 0912hrs: *Tone* joins with *Haguro*.

35. 0915hrs: Three Japanese destroyers fire torpedoes from long range at Taffy 3.

36. 1005hrs: *Samuel B. Roberts* sinks.

37. 1010hrs: *Johnston* sinks.

38. 1018hrs: *Chokai* scuttled.

39. 1100hrs: Torpedoes aboard *Suzuya* explode leading to her loss.

40. 1100hrs: *Chikuma* scuttled.

41. 1125hrs: *St. Lo* sinks after kamikaze attack.

Note: gridlines are shown at 5NM intervals.

Japanese. With the firepower available to him, Kurita planned to cripple the carriers with long-range battleship and heavy cruiser gunnery, followed by a mop-up attack with his destroyers. However, because of the smoke and squalls, the battleships were only able to fire at the carriers spasmodically. At 0730hrs, Kurita sent a message that he was engaging six carriers, including three fleet carriers. He held his destroyers back to maintain their fuel reserves by not having them maneuver at high speeds and sent his heavy cruisers ahead to pursue at full speed.

The result of this confusion was that by 0750hrs Kurita's force was spread out. *Kumano* and *Suzuya* were to the west, out of the battle. When Taffy 3 headed south, Kurita was slow to react and his ships did not turn south until around 0800hrs. The Japanese speed advantage eventually began to pay off. *Haruna*, *Kongo*, and the four remaining heavy cruisers were steering southeast and were for the most part clear of the smoke. *Haruna* spotted Taffy 2 to the southeast and briefly engaged that new target from 18NM, instead of maintaining fire against Taffy 3. The Japanese cruisers continued to gain, but after about 0845hrs, American aircraft concentrated on this threat. Soon, *Chikuma* and *Chokai* were both knocked out of action. This left only *Tone* and *Haguro*, and by 0920hrs they had closed the range to 8,000 yards. Apparently on his own initiative, late in the battle the commander of the 10th Torpedo Flotilla launched a torpedo attack at long range with no success.

It is clear that Kurita never understood the kind of battle he was fighting. The Japanese could not even decide what kind of carriers they were facing, since the silhouettes they observed were not in their recognition material. They ultimately decided they were facing regular carriers, though after the battle changed this assessment to converted carriers. The escorts were

Chikuma photographed from *Kalinin Bay* in the later stages of the action. This is one of the few times that an American and a Japanese ship are visible in the same image. At this point, *Chikuma* was some 8,000 yards away from the escort carriers.

variously identified as heavy and light cruisers, and at one time a battleship was even observed. Because they could only slowly make up ground on the fleeing Americans, the Japanese assessed the USN force was making 30 knots. Throughout the action, Kurita experienced poor communications with his cruisers, making it unclear what they were doing. Kurita's staff was concerned with the fuel states of their ships, particularly the destroyers.

What Sprague considered to be tactics of desperation to avoid annihilation, the Japanese assessed as tactical excellence. Kurita stated that the American destroyers had fought effectively and that they broke up his formation with torpedo attacks. His chief of staff commented that the destroyers "coordinated perfectly" and used smoke screens to great effect. Both judged American air attacks as incessant, aggressive, skillful, and well coordinated. In their view, they were the most skillful attacks encountered by the First Diversion Attack Force during the entire battle.

KURITA'S CONTROVERSIAL DECISION

The Battle off Samar essentially ended at 0911hrs when Kurita issued orders to break off the action. It took two hours to re-form his force. Once accomplished, Kurita ordered his 15 remaining ships to head southeast to Leyte Gulf, which was only 45NM away. After sending a message to Toyoda at 1205hrs stating his intent to penetrate into the gulf, at 1235hrs he reversed course. At 1310hrs his force passed near the area of the battle with Taffy 3 and continued north. With the door to Leyte Gulf open, Kurita changed his mind. What happened?

Even after the losses from the morning, after re-forming the First Diversion Attack Force was still a powerful formation. All four battleships were in fighting condition with plenty of ammunition. The once-formidable force of ten heavy cruisers had been whittled down to only two—*Tone* and *Haguro*. Light cruisers *Yahagi* and *Noshiro* led a force of nine destroyers, this number having been reduced after Kurita dispatched *Fujinami* and *Nowaki* to assist *Chikuma* and *Chokai*.

There are many reasons explaining Kurita's decision to turn back and forego the ultimate objective of *Sho-1* and any kind of Pyrrhic victory for the Imperial Navy. The first was his assessment that overwhelming forces were gathering to complete the destruction of his force. Kurita believed that his force had just tangled with part of the Third Fleet. During the action, another carrier task force had been spotted to the southeast, probably more elements of the Third Fleet. During the battle, Sprague and Kinkaid were active in communications, pleading in the clear for help from Halsey. These seemed to indicate that more forces were already near Leyte Gulf or on their way. These assumptions about the Third Fleet gained traction since Kurita had heard nothing of Ozawa's success in drawing Halsey's force to attack the Main Body. Furthermore, Kurita was aware that his Third Section had been annihilated trying to enter Leyte Gulf that morning.

Kurita probably held a fatalistic view of his prospects for survival as part of the *Sho-1* plan. This view was probably shared by all other officers of the fleet. Kurita and his men did not mind dying, but they wanted their deaths to count for something. Even before the departure of the First Diversion Attack Force from Brunei, there was open discontent at having to sacrifice the fleet, which represented the cream of the Imperial Navy, for mere transports. No doubt Kurita shared this sentiment. He was smart enough to realize that after the encounter with Taffy 3 the Americans would move any valuable ships out of the gulf, if they had not already done so. An aircraft from *Nagato* flew over Leyte Gulf and reported at 1235hrs that there were 35 transports in the gulf, not a lucrative invasion fleet. Kurita's greatest fear, which was shared by his chief of staff, was that his force would find itself in Leyte Gulf with nothing to attack, or at least nothing

In this image, an Avenger from *Kadashan Bay* approaches *Yamato* at an altitude of 1,500ft. Despite the attention from American aircraft on October 25, *Yamato* suffered no damage.

Tone was one of the most aggressive Japanese ships during the engagement, eventually closing to within 8,000 yards of Taffy 3's escort carriers and bringing them under effective fire. She was hit by a single 5in. shell during the action. This image is from a Kitkun Bay Avenger around 1240hrs when the cruiser was hit by a 500lb bomb that temporarily placed her steering gear out of action. Tone lost 19 men during the battle, but survived. The smoke in the image is from the ship's antiaircraft fire.

valuable to attack, and then be trapped and annihilated by American air power and surface ships. About the same time he was deciding whether to press south, he received reports of an American carrier force to the northeast. This report was false, but it gave Kurita an excuse for breaking off the advance south. Better to fight carriers than empty transports. Kurita's extreme mental and physical fatigue, which he admitted to after the battle, must also be taken into consideration. His entire staff concurred with the decision not to press the attack into the gulf.

In the final analysis, the contradictions of the ill-conceived *Sho-1* plan were so marked that not even a hard-bitten veteran like Kurita could live with them. Kurita's wartime record showed he was no coward. The events of the past three days during which he and his force had been subjected to relentless submarine, air, and surface attack made clear his fate if he pressed into Leyte Gulf. In the end, Kurita declined self-immolation for no purpose. By doing so he saved the lives of most of the approximately 15,000 men left aboard the First Diversion Attack Force. At 1236hrs, he signaled his intent to Toyoda to abandon the attack into Leyte Gulf.

THE FLIGHT OF THE FIRST DIVERSION ATTACK FORCE

After deciding to retreat, Kurita's ordeal was not over. Landing on *Manila Bay* in Taffy 2, Commander Richard L. Fowler (VC-5) took off again at 1100hrs and headed north to attack Kurita's retreating force. For this attack, he gathered some 16 Avengers escorted by a similar number of Wildcats. Another group of equal strength was under the direction of the officer commanding *Kadashan Bay*'s air group. Their attack began at 1245hrs and inflicted minor damage on *Nagato* and *Tone*. Taffy 2 launched its final attack of the day just after 1500hrs with 26 Avengers and 24 Wildcats. By this time, Kurita's force was 135NM away. This strike failed to inflict any damage on the fleeing Japanese.

Better results were expected from TG 38.1. This was the most powerful of Halsey's carrier task groups, with fleet carriers *Wasp*, *Hornet*, and *Hancock*, and light carriers *Cowpens* and *Monterey*. After breaking off refueling, it was steaming west at high speed to get within range of Kurita's fleet. When the strike was launched at 1045hrs, Kurita was some 335NM away, making this one of the longest carrier strikes of the war. The strike consisted of 48 Hellcats, 33 Helldivers, and 19 Avengers with bombs instead of torpedoes. Reaching the target at about 1315hrs, the strike placed only a single hit on *Tone*, but the bomb failed to explode.

Hornet and *Hancock* put in another strike at 1500hrs with 20 Hellcats, 20 Helldivers, and 13 Avengers. This attack also failed—not a single hit was recorded. McCain's aviators had flown over 150 sorties with no result. The aviators on the escort carriers, largely untrained for attacking ships, had performed much better.

Yamato and the remaining units of the First Diversion Attack Force came under attack on October 26 while retreating through the Sibuyan Sea. At about 1040hrs, Kurita's force came under attack from 30 Thirteenth Army Air Force B-24 "Liberators" from Morotai. Both *Yamato* and *Nagato* opened fire at the high-altitude bombers with their main armament using Type 3 *sanshikidan* shells. No bombers were hit, but as usual the B-24s also missed. However, bomb fragments did wound Kurita's chief of staff and about 60 others.

Heavy cruiser *Kumano* was attacked by *Hancock* aircraft on October 26, 1944. She had lost her bow the previous day at the hands of *Johnston*, and in this attack, she was hit by an additional three bombs. Note the SB2C Helldiver at right.

Unless the bulk of the Third Fleet could intervene, Kurita looked assured of escaping through the San Bernardino Strait. In a last effort to block the strait, Halsey detached the fastest ships from his battle line at 1622hrs. Designated TG 34.5, and comprised of battleships *Iowa*, *New Jersey*, light cruisers *Biloxi*, *Vincennes*, and *Miami*, along with eight destroyers, this small but powerful force raced ahead to beat the Japanese to the strait. They were too late. At 2140hrs, a night aircraft from *Independence* spotted Kurita's force filing through San Bernardino Strait. The only ship not to make it was destroyer *Nowaki* loaded with survivors from *Chikuma*. The overloaded destroyer was detected by the three light cruisers and three destroyers at 0054hrs on October 26 and quickly finished off.

As Kurita's force transited the Sibuyan Sea on October 26, Halsey planned another major strike from TG 38.1 and TG 38.2. Both groups launched strikes at 0600hrs, and McCain followed with two more. In total during the day, TG 38.2 put up 83 aircraft and TG 38.1 another 174. This was a comparable effort to that on October 24 that resulted in *Musashi*'s destruction.

Despite this level of effort, the results were meager. *Kumano* was hit by aircraft from *Hancock* between 0810hrs and 0850hrs. The strike consisted of 12 Hellcats, four Helldivers, and seven Avengers. Japanese accounts stated the cruiser was hit by three bombs that knocked out seven of eight boilers. After emergency repairs, *Kumano* succeeded in reaching Manila. After more repairs, she was sent home, but was attacked by four USN submarines on November 6. On November 25, the cruiser was attacked by aircraft from *Ticonderoga* in Santa Cruz Harbor on western Luzon. Hit by as many as five torpedoes and four bombs, *Kumano* capsized.

Aircraft from *Wasp* and *Cowpens* also found Kurita's main force. *Noshiro* was able to evade six torpedoes aimed at her, but at 0852hrs one struck with devastating effect. The ship lost all power and within minutes developed a 26° list to port. The next attack was conducted by aircraft from

A Yugumo-class destroyer photographed under attack from USN carrier aircraft off southern Mindoro on October 26, 1944 as Kurita's force headed west toward Brunei. The image was taken by an aircraft from light carrier *Cowpens*.

Hornet. A second torpedo hit the lightly protected cruiser at 1039hrs, and at 1113hrs she sank bow first.

By this point, Kurita's destroyers were down to their last few tons of fuel, forcing them to reduce speed. Destroyers had to shift fuel among themselves to reach a tanker positioned at Coron Bay. *Hayashimo* was forced to temporarily anchor off Semirara Island south of Mindoro. She was attacked by Avengers from 1045hrs to 1050hrs, and had her bow blown off by a torpedo. The next day, *Fujinami* was hit at 0920hrs while trying to assist. The destroyer broke in half and sank. Destroyer *Shiranui* was also sunk by dive-bombers around 1330hrs trying to render assistance. The crews of both ships, and the entire crew of *Chokai* aboard *Fujinami*, were all lost. *Hayashimo* later settled in shallow water and was lost. Five other destroyers (*Hamanami*, *Kishinami*, *Akishimo*, *Shimakaze*, and *Urakaze*) reached Coron Bay and refueled. The battleships, cruisers, and destroyers *Isokaze* and *Yukikaze* (both refueled by battleships) went to Brunei Bay by way of the Dangerous Ground (instead of the Palawan Passage) where they arrived on October 28.

THE ADVENT OF THE KAMIKAZE

The last phases of the Battle of Leyte Gulf witnessed another landmark event—the first organized Japanese suicide aircraft attack. Admiral Onishi had long been advocating for the initiation of formal suicide tactics. Throughout the war, Japanese pilots had crashed their aircraft on American ships on the spur of the moment. Now for the first time, Japanese pilots were sent into battle with the express intent of doing this. In Onishi's view, and many others, the futility of conventional attacks left the Japanese no choice.

Having organized the first kamikaze unit on October 20, it was not until October 25 that a kamikaze mission found suitable targets. By fate and not design, the first target was the American escort carrier force. Taffy 1 was located some 130NM to the south of Taffy 3 and thus was not engaged in the Battle off Samar. It was the target of the first group of six suicide aircraft that launched from Davao on Mindanao and headed north. Taffy 1 consisted of three Sangamon-class escort carriers and one Casablanca-class escort carrier, plus escorts. The Sangamons were converted oilers with the capacity to take much greater damage than the escort carriers converted from smaller cargo ships. The suicide aircraft, all A6M5 Zeros, were detected on radar, but not spotted through the scattered clouds as they approached their targets. The first ship to be attacked was *Santee*. At 0740hrs, a kamikaze commenced its dive, gained complete surprise, and encountered no antiaircraft fire before hitting the ship forward on the flight deck. Fires from the resulting explosion were quickly put out, but not before 43 men had been killed or wounded. Within five minutes of the fires being extinguished, submarine *I-56* slammed a torpedo into the ship. The converted tanker shook it off with no casualties and no loss of capability.

The second kamikaze selected *Suwannee* for attack. The Zero was hit by antiaircraft fire and crashed into the sea. A third Zero went after *Petrof Bay* but was also dispatched by antiaircraft fire. The final aircraft also selected *Petrof Bay* but ended up going after *Suwannee* after it was damaged by antiaircraft fire. It struck the carrier on the flight deck forward of the aft aircraft elevator. The Zero's 551lb bomb exploded, creating a hole on the hangar deck. The fires were put out within minutes, and within two hours flight operations had resumed.

Next to experience a full-blown kamikaze attack was battered Taffy 3. The suicide pilots approached the remaining five escort carriers at low level before popping up to altitude a few miles from their target. At this point they were detected on radar, but no interception by defending Wildcats was possible. At 1049hrs, *Kitkun Bay* was attacked by a single Zero. The pilot failed to hit the carrier's bridge, but his aircraft hit the port-side catwalk before crashing into the sea. The ship incurred damage when the Zero's bomb exploded close alongside. Two more suicide aircraft were dispatched by antiaircraft fire. The last two Zeros selected *White Plains* for their attentions. One came in from astern but missed the ship after crashing into the water close aboard the port side. The other was deterred by antiaircraft fire and headed toward *St. Lo*.

In this remarkable image, *Suwannee* is hit by a kamikaze on October 25, 1944. The lack of antiaircraft fire indicates the Japanese aircraft has gained some measure of surprise. On the left is an F6F Hellcat pulling out of the dive after chasing the suicide aircraft. This photograph was taken from *Petrof Bay*.

St. Lo was the first USN ship sunk by suicide attack. This is the moment the ship's magazine exploded, resulting in her loss on October 25, 1944.

The last kamikaze was the most skillful. At 1053hrs, the Zero came in over the stern of *St. Lo* and dropped his bomb before performing a shallow dive into the flight deck amidships. The aircraft slid off the bow, leaving a trail of fire on the flight deck from its fuel. The fire was no problem to deal with, but the bomb penetrated the flight deck and exploded in the hangar deck, where six aircraft were being fueled and armed. The resulting explosion forced the ship to be abandoned, and 32 minutes after being struck, the ship sank with 114 crewmen after the fires reached its magazines. *St. Lo* was the first ship sunk by kamikaze attack.

At 1110hrs, another four kamikazes appeared and selected *Kalinin Bay* for attack. Two were shot down by antiaircraft fire. The other pair both scored glancing hits. One Zero was hit by antiaircraft fire, remained in control, and then hit the flight deck at a shallow angle and slid overboard. The second hit the ship with a glancing blow aft.

The next day, the kamikazes returned to attack Taffy 1. Three Zeros penetrated the CAP and attacked *Suwannee*, which had completed repairs from the prior day's suicide attack. One Zero hit the flight deck and smashed into a group of ten aircraft parked on the bow. The aircraft were quickly engulfed in flames that spread down into the hangar bay, where another ten fueled aircraft were preparing to be brought up to the flight deck. The resulting fires on the hangar deck were put out, followed two hours later by the fire on the flight deck. The crew paid a high price for saving their ship— 85 dead, 58 missing, and 102 wounded. Other kamikazes selected *Sangamon* and *Petrof Bay* for attack; both carriers reported being near-missed.

The apparent success of the first kamikaze attacks provided the Japanese with the hope they had found a way to stop the American naval onslaught. A handful of aircraft had sunk one escort carrier and damaged five others to varying degrees. October 25 witnessed the Imperial Navy's last fleet action, and also a desperate new tactic the Japanese used extensively for the remainder of the war.

AFTERMATH

The heart of *Sho-1* was the charge of the First Diversion Attack Force into Leyte Gulf. Kurita's force failed in its mission, making the entire operation a failure. In the course of its operations from October 22 to 27, the First Diversion Attack Force paid a high price for this.

Table 4: Losses suffered by the First Diversion Attack Force, October 22–27, 1944

Ship type	At start	Sunk	Severely damaged	Remaining
Battleships	5	1	0	4
Heavy cruisers	10	5	3	2
Light cruisers	2	1	0	1
Destroyers	15	3	0	12
Total	**32**	**10**	**3**	**19**

In addition to the ships lost, total personnel casualties from Kurita's ships were over 5,000 killed.

After the operation, the IJN no longer existed as a force capable of large-scale operations. Kurita's remaining ships went to Brunei Bay and then on to Lingga Roads. Keeping the fleet there was impossible. While fuel was relatively plentiful, there was no ammunition and only limited repair facilities. Over the next several weeks, most ships returned to the Home Islands.

Of the four battleships, all but one reached Japan. The exception was *Kongo*, sunk by submarine *Sealion* in the Formosa Strait on November 21. *Yamato*, the IJN's last remaining prestige ship, reached Japan on November 23. In an operation even more pointless than *Sho-1*, she was sent on a suicidal mission to attack American forces off Okinawa on April 6, 1945. The next day, she was pounded under the waves by American carrier aircraft, with 3,056 of her crew killed. *Haruna* and *Nagato* also reached home waters, but the lack of fuel kept them inactive for the rest of the war. *Haruna* was sunk by carrier air attack on July 28, 1945, leaving *Nagato* as the only Japanese battleship to survive the war.

In the aftermath of Leyte Gulf, the IJN was rendered incapable of major fleet operations. The last significant IJN operation was the pointless sacrifice of *Yamato* in April 1945 following the American invasion of Okinawa. Just as *Musashi* was sunk by carrier aircraft in October 1944, *Yamato* was ordered to approach Okinawa without air cover and was sunk in the same manner. This huge explosion marks the end of *Yamato* on April 7, 1945.

American survivors of the Battle off Samar spent as much as three days in the water awaiting rescue. Some 1,200 survivors from the four USN ships lost in the battle were rescued during the days following the action. Here, some survivors are picked up on October 26, 1944.

Of the 12 cruisers assigned to Kurita's force, only two returned to Japan. *Tone* was sunk by American carrier aircraft in port on July 29, 1945. *Yahagi* accompanied *Yamato* on her last sortie and was sunk with the loss of 446 men. *Haguro* remained in southern waters and was tracked down by Royal Navy forces on May 16, 1945 on a mission to remove the garrison from the Andaman Islands. Her destruction southwest of Penang was the final major action by a Japanese combatant during the war.

In comparison, USN losses were much lower, but were still significant. The all-out Japanese effort to neutralize TF 38 on October 24, 1944 came up short of its objective. However, it did account for light carrier *Princeton* and extensive topside damage to light cruiser *Birmingham*. A total of 337

The losses suffered by the USN at the Battle of Leyte Gulf were minor and in no way hindered future operations. This is *Kalinin Bay* arriving at San Diego, California on November 25, 1944 for repairs to damage received in the Battle off Samar a month earlier.

men were lost on these two ships. Meanwhile, while attacking Kurita's force on October 24, TF 38 lost only 18 aircraft.

TG 77.4 took the brunt of the USN losses during the battle. Between its battle with the First Diversion Attack Force and kamikazes, losses were severe. In addition to two escort carriers, two destroyers, and a destroyer escort sunk, personnel losses were high with 311 killed, 677 missing, and 914 wounded.

Whatever losses the USN suffered during the battle had no impact whatsoever on its ability to support the invasion of Leyte. TF 38 remained on station after the battle. On October 29–30, 1944 it was struck by a wave of kamikazes. *Intrepid* was hit on the first day, followed by *Franklin* and *Belleau Wood* the following day. TF 38 finally retired to Ulithi on October 30.

In the final analysis, the *Sho-1* plan was utterly without hope. Toyoda knew it as soon as it was created, and every other Japanese naval officer with any insight knew it as well. The man ultimately responsible for carrying out this act of idiocy declined to sacrifice his men for no other purpose than to uphold the Imperial Navy's peculiar brand of honor. Of all the Japanese command decisions of the battle, Kurita's was the most courageous. The failure of *Sho-1* left the Japanese with no fleet and no hope of defeating the USN. What followed was another act of moral cowardice by turning to suicide operations. It was soon apparent that these could cause mayhem and death but could not stop the USN or change the course of the war.

The fact that *Sho-1* had elements of cleverness that exposed seams in the USN's command structure should not disguise the fact that it had absolutely no chance of success and was nothing more than a vessel for the IJN's immolation. Even if Kurita had pressed into Leyte Gulf, it would have resulted in no meaningful military advantage for the Japanese and would have surely meant the total annihilation of Kurita's force. The myth that Leyte Gulf was a battle the Japanese could have won, and in fact could have won if not for the indecision of one man, needs to be put to rest.

BIBLIOGRAPHY

Como, Byron G., *The Defenders of Taffy 3*, Print on Demand (2018)

Cox, Robert J., *The Battle off Samar* (5th Ed.), Agogeebic Press, Wakefield, Michigan (2010)

Dull, Paul S., *A Battle History of the Imperial Japanese Navy (1941–1945)*, Naval Institute Press, Annapolis, Maryland (1978)

Falk, Stanley L., *Decision at Leyte*, W. W. Norton and Company, New York (1966)

Field, James A., *The Japanese at Leyte Gulf*, Princeton University Press, London (1947)

Fletcher, Gregory G., *Intrepid Aviators*, NAL Caliber, New York (2012)

Friedman, Kenneth I., *Afternoon of the Rising Sun*, Presidio Press, Novato, California (2001)

Hornfischer, James D., *The Last Stand of the Tin Can Sailors*, Bantam Books, New York (2004)

Hoyt, Edwin P., *The Battle of Leyte Gulf*, Weybright and Talley, New York (1972)

Ito, Masanori, *The End of the Imperial Japanese Navy*, W. W. Norton and Company, New York (1962)

Japanese Monograph No. 82, *Philippines Area Naval Operations, Part I Jan.–Sep. 1944*, General Headquarters Supreme Commander for the Allied Powers (1947)

Japanese Monograph No. 84, *Philippines Area Naval Operations, Part II Oct.–Dec. 1944*, General Headquarters Supreme Commander for the Allied Powers (1947)

Lacroix, Eric and Wells, Linton, *Japanese Cruisers of the Pacific War*, Naval Institute Press, Annapolis, Maryland (1997)

Lundgren, Robert, *The World Wonder'd: What Really Happened off Samar*, Nimble Books, Ann Arbor, Michigan (2014)

Mansfield, John G., *Cruisers for Breakfast*, Media Center Publishing, Tacoma, Washington (1997)

Morison, Samuel Eliot, *History of United States Naval Operations in World War II*, Vol. XII: *Leyte June 1944–January 1945*, Little, Brown and Company, Boston (1974)

O'Hara, Vincent P., *The U.S. Navy Against the Axis*, Naval Institute Press, Annapolis, Maryland (2007)

Prados, John, *Storm Over Leyte*, NAL Caliber, New York (2016)

Reynolds, Clark, *The Fast Carriers*, Naval Institute Press, Annapolis, Maryland (1992)

Sears, David, *The Last Epic Naval Battle*, Praeger, Westport, Connecticut (2005)

Solberg, Carl, *Decision and Dissent*, Naval Institute Press, Annapolis, Maryland (1995)

Southwest Pacific Area Command, *Japanese Operations in the Southwest Pacific Area*, Vol. II, Part II, Tokyo (1950)

Thomas, Evan, *Sea of Thunder*, Simon & Schuster, New York (2006)

Thornton, Tim, "Air Power: The Sinking of IJN Battleship Musashi," *Warship XII*, Naval Institute Press, Annapolis (1991)

United States Strategic Bombing Survey (Pacific), *The Campaigns of the Pacific War*, United States Government Printing Office, Washington (1946)

United States Strategic Bombing Survey (Pacific), *Interrogations of Japanese Officials* (Vol. I), United States Government Printing Office, Washington (n. d.)

Willmott, H. P., *The Battle of Leyte Gulf*, Indiana University Press, Bloomington (2005)

Woodward, C. Vann, *The Battle for Leyte Gulf*, W. W. Norton and Company, New York (1947)

Website: www.combinedfleet.com

INDEX

Figures in **bold** refer to illustrations and maps.